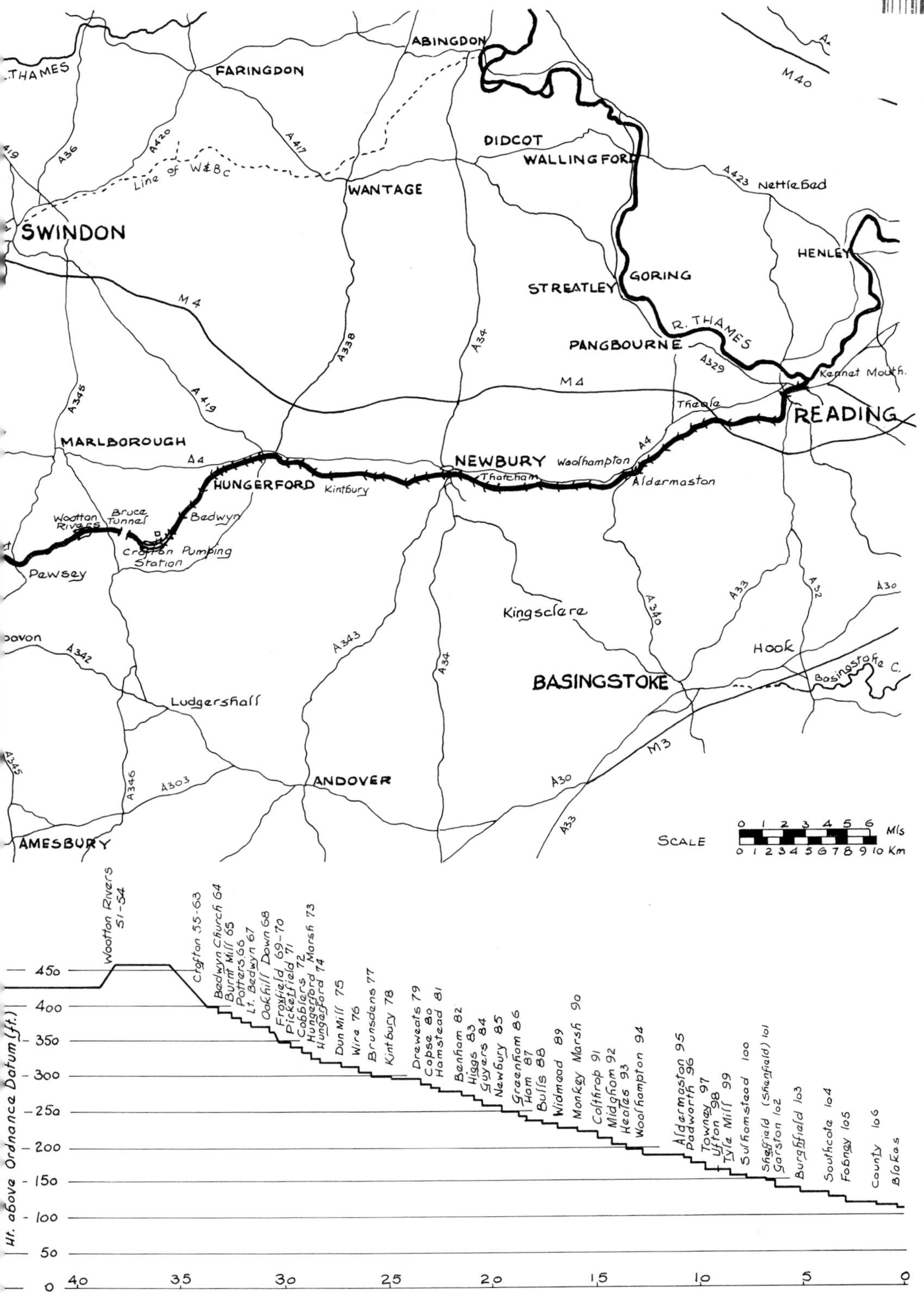
THAMES
FARINGDON
ABINGDON
M40
DIDCOT
WALLINGFORD
A423 Nettlebed
Line of W&BC
WANTAGE
SWINDON
HENLEY
STREATLEY
GORING
R. THAMES
PANGBOURNE
Kennet Mouth
M4
Theale
READING
MARLBOROUGH
NEWBURY
Woolhampton
Thatcham
Aldermaston
HUNGERFORD
Kintbury
Bedwyn
Wootton Rivers
Bruce Tunnel
Crofton Pumping Station
Pewsey
Kingsclere
Hook
BASINGSTOKE
Basingstoke C.
Ludgershall
ANDOVER
AMESBURY
SCALE
Mls
Km
Ht. above Ordnance Datum (ft.)
Wootton Rivers 51-54
Crofton 55-63
Bedwyn Church 64
Burnt Mill 65
Potters 66
Lt. Bedwyn 67
Oakhill Down 68
Froxfield 69-70
Picketfield 71
Cobblers 72
Hungerford Marsh 73
Hungerford 74
Dun Mill 75
Wire 76
Brunsdens 77
Kintbury 78
Dreweats 79
Copse 80
Hamstead 81
Benham 82
Higgs 83
Guyers 84
Newbury 85
Greenham 86
Ham 87
Bulls 88
Widmead 89
Monkey Marsh 90
Colthrop 91
Midgham 92
Heales 93
Woolhampton 94
Aldermaston 95
Padworth 96
Towney 97
Ufton 98
Tyle Mill 99
Sulhamstead 100
Sheffield (Shenfield) 101
Garston 102
Burghfield 103
Southcote 104
Fobney 105
County 106
Blakes

The Kennet & Avon Canal

A Journey from Newbury to Bath in 1964

(above) The view north-west through Crofton Lock, No.55, towards the abutments of the bridge carrying the former Midland & South West Junction Railway across the canal.
(opposite) Brimslade Bridge and Wootton Rivers Lock, No.53.

The Kennet & Avon Canal

A Journey from Newbury to Bath in 1964

John Russell

Millstream Books

this book
is respectfully dedicated to
Roger Hardy
who introduced me to canals

Orchard Meadow Bridge, near Kintbury

First published in 1997 by Millstream Books, 18 The Tyning, Bath BA2 6AL

Set in GillSans Light and printed in Great Britain by The Matthews Wright Press, Chard

ISBN 0 948975 46 6

British Library Cataloguing-in-Publication Data: a catalogue record for this book is available from The British Library

Foreword

'Yours to enjoy' is a slogan used by British Waterways for the Kennet & Avon Canal, whose survival is due to the K&A Canal Asociation (subsequently K&A Canal Trust) and others. When John Russell made his towpath journey in 1964 the waterway had suffered decades of neglect, and navigation was limited to short lengths at Newbury, the summit level and Bath. His book is a unique description in words and pictures of the faded glory of 'The Sleeping Beauty' of the waterways and is essential reading for all interested in the K&A. Soon after its reopening in 1990 by Her Majesty The Queen, the K&A Canal Partnership was formed by the K&A Canal Trust, riparian Local Authorities and British Waterways. In 1996 the Partnership was granted £25 million by the Heritage Lottery Fund to resolve major structural problems of instability and water supply. Though the canal's future seems assured, John Russell's book is a timely reminder of how much needed to be done to bring it back to use and that

"nothing great was ever achieved without enthusiasm"

(Ralph Waldo Emerson)

Kenneth R. Clew
June 1997

Contents

Preface 6
Background History 7
The Journey 11
Stone Supplies 106
Canalia 113
Condition of the Structures in 1964 117
Glossary 130
Bibliography 133
Acknowledgements 134
Index 135

Preface

When I was planning this study, my idea was to include a photograph and description of every work of architectural interest along the length of the canal. Starting out by bicycle from Newbury one frosty October morning in 1964, I soon realised that there were more works of architectural interest than I had bargained for. Eight rolls of film and four days later, I arrived in Bath, saddle-sore and sated with canal scenery. A few of the photographs did not come up to expectations and this necessitated a further trip to selected parts of the canal, this time by scooter. There were further trips to various places along the canal; to Bath, Hungerford, Crofton and Newbury, before I was satisfied that my set of photos was complete. Long before then, it was apparent that with more than 360 black and white photographs and 40 colour slides, taken on visits to the canal in earlier years, the idea of including so many pictures in one book was out of the question.

The arrangement I worked out was to give an introductory background history, followed by a conducted journey along the canal from Newbury to Bath. To assist those completely foreign to the subject, I then added a glossary which included words and phrases in the text not in common usage, and which should prove useful when certain sections are reached. For the seriously interested, the appendix lists every observed work of architectural or engineering merit on the canal from my own first-hand observations of its condition in 1964.

But with the passing of years, the thesis on which this book was based has become of increasing interest as a 'Snapshot in Time', as a record of a romantic ruin prior to restoration. Back in 1964, I didn't imagine in my wildest dreams that, well within my lifetime, this canal would be fully restored, with marinas and several hire boat companies based along it.

The fascination I find in canals and inland waterways is that there are so many different aspects of the subject – surveying, architecture, water supply, boat building, boat handling, flora and fauna associated with water, social history, etc, that anyone with an enquiring mind can be led down unexpected yet enjoyable byways. It is tempting to believe that everything to be found close to the canal has been there since the day it was opened, but of course this is not so. Bridges have been altered or improved, railway lines have been recycled for use as stop plank racks, and safety railings have appeared in the Sydney Gardens tunnels, for example. If, by reading this book you are encouraged to get out there, to look, to understand and perhaps to discover more about our heritage of industrial archaeology, then my efforts will have been worthwhile.

John Russell, Northampton, Spring 1997

Background History

The River Kennet was made navigable from the Thames at Reading to Newbury as early as 1723, but it was not until late December 1810 that the canal joining Newbury to the River Avon Navigation at Bath was finally open for trade. The Avon was made navigable some time earlier, the first barge arriving in Bath in December 1727. In the Spring of 1788 various parties interested in joining the rivers Kennet and Avon met to discuss the problem and cost involved in such a vast project.

Originally called the Western Canal and planned only to join Hungerford to Newbury, this was soon seen to be inadequate, and three engineers, Barns, Simcock and Weston, were commissioned to make a survey of a through route from Newbury to Bath. In 1789 their reports were submitted to Robert Whitworth for approval, who reported favourably to the committee for a line to run via Hungerford, Marlborough and Calne, although he queried the adequacy of the water supply to the summit. The Western Canal committee then decided to have a further survey made by John Rennie, who was subsequently appointed Engineer to the canal on the 20th May, 1794. The committee, on 3rd November 1790:

> Resolved Unanimously That a Junction of the Rivers Kennett [sic] and Avon, by a Canal Navigation from Newbury to Bath, by Hungerford, Ramsbury, Marlborough, and the Cherrill lower Level, under the White-Horse Hill, and through Calne, Chippenham, Laycock, Melksham, and Bradford, at the estimated Expence of 213,940£ is practicable, and will be highly useful and beneficial to the Subscribers, and to the Publick at large.

A prospectus was then issued and subscription lists opened. The money came in slowly at first but, by 1793, subscriptions had reached almost £1 million and Rennie was instructed to make a full survey and pass his findings to Whitworth, who was advising the committee. Approaches were made to the Kennet Navigation, the Thames Commissioners, the City of London, and the River Avon proprietors.

In July 1793 Rennie proposed a revised route via Hungerford, Great Bedwyn and Devizes, to Bradford and Bath, with branches to Marlborough, Calne and Chippenham as he was doubtful if the earlier route would have a sufficient water supply. This would involve building a 4,312-yard tunnel at Savernake. *The Kennet & Avon Canal Act* received the Royal Assent on 17th April 1794. One of Rennie's first tasks was to make a survey of the comparative costs of constructing a wide canal for boats of 50 tons, compared to a narrow canal of 25 tons. William Jessop, a fellow canal engineer, was asked to make a similar survey. He agreed with

Rennie's report and estimates, but proposed a slight route change, which would lead the summit pound through a long cutting instead of a tunnel. This was the chosen route, although Thomas Bruce, Earl of Ailesbury, insisted on the canal being hidden from view by means of a short tunnel. Jessop reckoned that a cutting would be cheaper than a long tunnel, even allowing for the additional cost of locks to raise the canal to a higher level, which required a steam engine to pump up water from Wilton to the shortened summit pound.

Earlier, in September 1793, the name of the project was changed to the Kennet & Avon Canal to avoid confusion with The Grand Western Canal which was planned to link the River Exe to Taunton. When *The Kennet & Avon Canal Act* was passed on 17th April 1794, £420,000 capital was authorised, with power to raise an additional £120,000. As will be shown later, this was a grossly optimistic estimate, the eventual cost being nearer £980,000, although this included the purchase of the Kennet Navigation and a controlling interest in the River Avon Navigation. A small saving had been made by the decision in January 1794 to omit the branch to Marlborough.

Work on the canal was started at Bradford-on-Avon and at Newbury in the same year, 1794, and proceeded with frequent setbacks and financial crises until completion in 1810. The Newbury to Hungerford section was completed in 1798, and that to Great Bedwyn the following year. The section from Bath to Foxhangers was partially completed at this stage, but not finished until 1804. In 1802, Foxhangers was connected to Devizes by a double-track iron railway, almost certainly a plate tramway using horses as motive power, until the Devizes locks were completed. The following year the Devizes to Pewsey section was being built, but that from Pewsey to Great Bedwyn had not been started. By December 1809 both these sections had been completed, with the exception of the great flight of 29 locks at Devizes and the flight of 7 locks at Bath. A passenger boat service was operating on the western section from Shrivenham on the Wilts and Berks Canal to the top of the uncompleted Widcombe flight in Bath. As built, the canal from Newbury to Bath was broad-gauge, 40 feet wide at the top (44 feet on the summit level), to take barges 70 feet by 13 feet 6 inches, loading 50 tons. The line was 57 miles long, with 79 locks (in addition to the six on the Avon between Bath and Bristol), each 80 feet long by 14 feet wide, with a draught of 6 feet, two large aqueducts and various smaller ones, numerous culverts and one tunnel.

Two canals joined the main line, which developed into a mutually dependent waterway system. The more important of the two was the Somersetshire Coal Canal. Authorised in 1794, it ran from Limpley Stoke near Dundas Aqueduct to Midford, Combe Hay, Dunkerton, Camerton and Timsbury, with a tramroad branch from Midford to Wellow and Radstock. This canal tapped the Somerset coalfield and was a valuable source of revenue for the Kennet & Avon Canal. The other was the Wilts and Berks Canal, which ran from the K&A at

Semington to the Thames at Abingdon via Melksham, Wootton Bassett, Swindon, Shrivenham and Challow. This was 51 miles long with branches to Calne, Chippenham, Longcot for Faringdon, and Wantage. The canal was authorised in 1795 and open throughout in 1810, just three months before the Kennet & Avon Canal. The purpose of the Wilts and Berks was to convey Somerset coal to the Vale of the White Horse and bring away agricultural produce.

By the end of 1810 the Kennet & Avon, the Wilts and Berks and the Somersetshire Coal Canals were all open, and together they had a considerable effect on those living in the valleys of the River Avon and the Upper Thames above Reading. The single most important result was a reduction in the price of coal to places where it had been brought by costly land carriage before the cutting of the canals.

In 1812 the Kennet & Avon Canal Company bought the Kennet Navigation for £100,000 and two years later obtained six more shares in the Avon Navigation, in addition to those they had bought already, which then gave them a controlling interest. In the same year, the Company contributed £7,000 towards the cost of a towpath for the River Avon, to assist the through passage of horse-drawn traffic from London to Bristol. In 1814, the Kennet & Avon Canal Company paid its first dividend, for the trading year 1813. By 1818 seventy 60-ton barges were plying on the canal, the time taken to cover the 57 miles between Bath and Newbury averaging about three and a half days. Traffic increased and by 1832 there passed some 300,000 tons per annum, although, as on the Leeds and Liverpool, of this only a certain proportion passed over the summit. During the years 1825 to 1834, the annual revenue averaged about £45,000, but due to high initial costs the dividend averaged about 3½%.

With the advent of the Great Western Railway the canal faced severe competition, and whilst revenue rose to £58,820 in 1840 with the carrying of material for building the railway, the inevitable decline subsequently occurred and revenue was down to £30,857 by 1849. In 1842 the maintenance staff numbered 122, comprising 42 lock-keepers, 17 carpenters, 14 masons, 2 blacksmiths, 4 ballasters, 17 puddlers and 26 labourers. This staff was subsequently reduced to 100, and the toll by 25%, to only five shillings per ton from Bath to Reading. The staff then remained at almost 100 until nationalisation on 1st January, 1948. The GWR purchased the canal in 1852 with the object of eliminating competition to their railway.

The GWR, although they never actually closed the canal, discouraged boats, though these were occasionally passed through after some delay – mainly caused by lack of dredging. Section 17 of the *Regulation of Railways Act* of 1873 required railway companies that had bought canals to maintain them in a navigable condition, so maintenance was kept just within the law. The GWR also prohibited powered craft on the canal without prior permission, though it is interesting to note that powered pleasure craft were not prohibited. They forbade weekend working, and in 1906 the Royal Commission on Inland Waterways was able to report that the tolls on the Kennet & Avon Canal were 50% higher than those on any other comparable waterway in the country. During the long periods of railway management the canal was kept navigable, although every method was used to discourage traffic from using it in favour of the railway. Routine maintenance work was carried out and although stoppages did occur, these were not of long duration. However, the maintenance was executed almost entirely in softwood timber, so that its useful life was considerably shorter than would have been the case if hardwood had been employed. It is said that the GWR paid a 'good ideas' bonus to the foreman who suggested using softwood instead of hardwood. Little or no attempt was made to improve any of the works of the canal. For instance, the majority of the swing bridges continued to be built in wood, and of the original pattern, instead of being made in steel of improved type. No attempt was made to replace any of the small accommodation swing bridges with overhead bridges, which both reduce ultimate maintenance costs and also facilitate the flow of water-borne traffic.

On 1st January 1948 the canal passed to the British Transport Commission as a result of the *Transport Act* of 1947 and a certain amount of restoration work was done to the architectural features. But this work was stopped soon afterwards, dredgers and workboats were transferred to other waterways, the maintenance staff was reduced and the waterway was systematically allowed to deteriorate. It has to be remembered, however, that in the post-war years the whole country was run down, there was a lack of manpower, with shortages of fuel and labour, so that work on the canal had a low priority.

An attempt was made in 1955 to abandon the canal legally, but this was defeated after stiff opposition from the Kennet & Avon Canal Association (as it then was), the Inland Waterways Association and numerous other interested bodies, but chiefly through the actions of John Gould, a working boatman and canal trader from Newbury, who sued the British Transport Commission and won damages of £5,000. A breach in the bank just west of Avoncliff Aqueduct in October 1954 led to a section being 'stopped off', from the pound between the stop gates just east of the aqueduct to those at Limpley Stoke, ostensibly for repairs to be carried out. No doubt British Railways was concerned about the safety of its line, which passed along the base of the canal embankment downstream of the aqueduct. In December 1963, the British Waterways Board under the chairmanship of Sir John Hawton stated in its Interim Report that "restoration merits sympathetic, careful and urgent consideration". After a long struggle by countless volunteers, working in partnership with BWB, the canal was eventually re-opened to through navigation by the Queen on 8th August 1990.

The Journey

In this chapter reference should be made to the map of the canal for the location of the various places mentioned, as the course is traced from Newbury to Bath.

The canal section of the whole waterway starts officially at Newbury Wharf. The first obstacle to horse-drawn boats heading west towards Bath is Town, or Water Bridge which has no towpath. This narrow stone bridge, built between 1769 and 1772 by James Clarke, carried the old Oxford to Southampton road over the Kennet, and is where my journey starts. A light line had to be floated downstream under the bridge, on an arrowhead-shaped wooden float. The line was then attached to the boat, for the horse to pull it up to the first lock not far away, Newbury Lock, No.85.

The chamber of Newbury Lock is of brick with the top of the chamber and approach walls capped with Bath stone, which acts as a blocking course and protects the brickwork from damage. The walls are slightly wider at the top than at the base, to attempt to alleviate the effects of frost expansion. This contributed to the damage wrought on the Lower Stratford Canal, especially on the Wilmcote flight, where every lock wall was found to have bulged inwards. The gates are of solid oak and there is one paddle for each gate, but the filling of the lock is helped by a ground paddle of the type common in the North of England, where they are known as cloughs, but rare in the south. A long paddle is pivoted below water level by means of a handle roughly four feet long, which lies horizontally when the paddle is in the closed position. The handrails are probably not original, possibly obtained from the Grand Union Canal Company, but are practical and, therefore, no doubt similar to those first fitted.

At West Mills the first of many swing bridges on the canal is encountered. This provides access from the road to the site of a former flour mill, still in production at the time of my journey but burnt down in c.1970 and converted into flats a few years later. Immediately beyond the bridge is a row of 17th-century houses known as the Weavers' Cottages and still occupied. There are several attractive Georgian houses worthy of note alongside the canal at this point.

Ensuring a constant level of water in his canal is a source of continual concern to the canal engineer. The possibility of leaks, blowouts in embankments and the results of damage by rivers in flood has to be allowed for and, if possible, protected against. Various devices were employed. In the section east of Hungerford where the River Kennet flows in and out of the canal, elaborate weirs have been built, such as that above, near Hamstead Marshall. Additional channels were made with their own sluice gear, operated by a handspike, for use in time of flood, as illustrated, near the same place.

The canal now follows the valley of the River Kennet through flat meadowland, the river never being far away. The locks as far as Hamstead Lock, No.81, but not including it, were in excellent condition, even in 1964, mainly as a result of the diligence of the local British Waterways inspector at that time, the late Cyril Rogers. They even include the iron stakes known as strapping posts, alongside the lock chambers, originally used to check horse-drawn boats when entering the lock, as in this view of Guyer's Lock, No.84. At Hamstead Marshall the river flows in and out of the canal in a maze of channels; there was a mill near the bridge in former years. Accompanying the river, the Bath road and the main railway line, the canal climbs in easy stages up the valley towards Hungerford.

There are a great number of brick bridges on the canal between Newbury and Devizes which have not been touched since the day they were built. Their architectural design and aesthetic effect is very satisfying. They fit into the landscape as if they have always been there, enhancing the scenery rather than detracting from it – as is so often the case with many of the iron structures of the railway age. Although simple to look at, there is a high level of workmanship in them all. They were built with the walls curved in plan view, these acting as arches springing from the buttress piers on either side of the arch. In addition, the walls are slightly concave, which makes them virtually indestructible as far as internal factors are concerned. The example above is Carrel Crown Bridge, near Wootton Rivers.

Rennie has been called "Pontifex Maximus" and certainly the number of bridges and aqueducts he was called on to design and build on the Kennet & Avon alone could qualify him for that title. Cyril T. G. Boucher, in his book *John Rennie, 1761-1821*, eulogises on his undoubted ability as an architect and engineer: "For handsome proportions, grace and beauty of line and delicacy of detail, they stand in a class apart; they have never been excelled and rarely equalled". Boucher's early training gave him a good understanding of the way in which Rennie combined the aesthetic and the functional in the design of his bridges and aqueducts, which are graceful, well-proportioned and built to last. Rennie, like Thomas Telford, was one of the old school of engineer architects, who could and often would complete the design of a whole bridge or any structure; unlike today, where the various professions are fragmented and so many different organisations become involved that the final edifice often proclaims itself as the work of a committee. One wonders why the aqueducts were not built in the same way; most of them have straight, vertical sides with iron tie bars below the bed of the canal, designed to take the outward thrust from the waterway. Wouldn't they have been stronger if they had imitated Rennie's standard bridge design, as in the view above of Benham Bridge?

At Kintbury is a canalside inn, *The Dundas Arms*, with its former stables now in use as garages. From an undated extract in the *Newbury Weekly News*, we read that:

> Charles Dundas, a Scot, married Ann Whitley in 1782. At that time he was sitting for Orkney and Shetland in the Commons. Miss Whitley was an heiress, and through her he came into possession of the manor of Kintbury-Amesbury. Barton Court was henceforth his home.

From this it seems likely that the inn assumed its present name after 1782. *Barton Court* lies to the north of Kintbury, between the river and the London to Bath road. Vicarage Bridge above the lock at Kintbury provides access to the Parish Church, in which can be found a memorial plaque to Charles Dundas, promoter and chairman for many years of the Kennet & Avon Canal Company.

Passing the hamlet of Avington, across the meadows to the right, the canal arrives at Dunmill Lock, No.75. Here was to be found the first of several brick dams built immediately behind the top gates, to retain the water in the pound above. These dams naturally prevented navigation and were, therefore, illegal, since the canal was never legally abandoned. However, they did prevent the various pounds from drying out, resulting in cracking of the clay puddle, which makes the canal watertight, and the destruction of fish and plant life; presumably the dams were cheaper to construct than new gates. Immediately above the lock the canal widens to form a mooring place and turning point, or winding hole, which was used by boats and barges waiting to load at Denford Mill.

A mile away is Hungerford (above), whose chief inhabitants met to discuss the possibility of the extension of the Kennet Navigation to their town way back in 1788, before the 'canal mania' began. Although to be fair to them, they did add "and as far further as shall hereafter be thought eligible". The Western Canal, as it was then called, subsequently grew into the Kennet & Avon Canal, as described earlier.

Two examples of cast-iron bridges worth noting exist at Hungerford (right). Although not strictly connected with the canal, they were erected to cross the towpath entrances, on either side of the A338 road bridge over the canal. They provided access to new front doors on the first floor of these two houses. The footbridge to the east of the bridge has a cast-iron deck supported by beams made up into a pattern of quatrefoils and elongated diamond shapes. The footbridge is approached through an archway and up some steps. The handrails are simple square bar, but have ring decorations at two places on each bar. The other footbridge is plainer. The footway is supported by two cast-iron girders and the handrails are made of shaped balusters, 18 on each side. As these are riveted to the top rail, which rules out cast-iron as the material used, it seems likely that they were machined on an elementary lathe. Just inside the entrance to St Lawrence's Church on the western outskirts of Hungerford is a memorial plaque to John Blackwell, Engineer to the canal for 34 years.

A mile above Hungerford Wharf at Hungerford Marsh Lock, No.73, is the first of the two swing bridges over a lock, on this canal, the other being over Burnt Mill Lock, No.65. In the former case an existing right of way was maintained, although this is hard to believe today. It is surprising that this utilisation of the narrowing of the canal channel by the lock walls should not have been used more often for a bridge. Other examples exist on various canals, as at Wheaton Aston Lock, No.2, on the Shropshire Union Canal and at Fenny Stratford Lock on the Grand Union Canal.

Many K&A swing bridges are still in use, the majority in reasonable condition. There are two main types, illustrated above:

(i) those suitable for normal farm traffic, as near Bathampton, and

(ii) those suitable for pedestrians only, as at All Cannings.

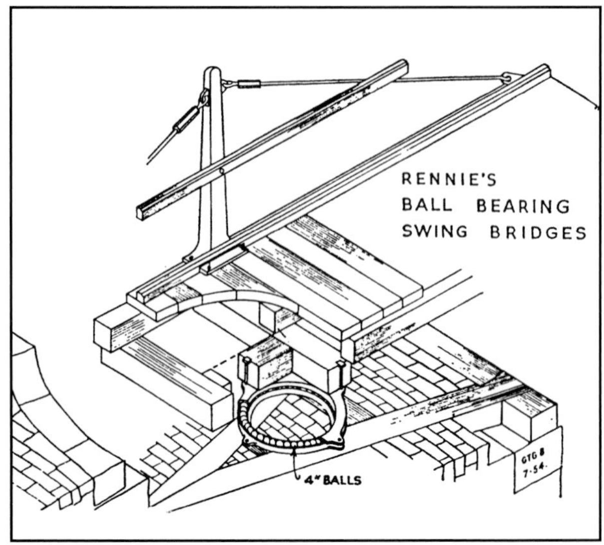

In some cases, wooden railings have been replaced by metal ones, as on a few near Melksham. Several swing bridges have been removed, but some have been completely rebuilt in the traditional pattern using the original suspension chains and bearings. These bridges were mounted on a wooden framework which was, in turn, mounted on a ball-race bolted to stout timbers embedded in the brickwork of the bridge foundations, as shown above at Bishops Cannings. Boucher (see page 17) puts forward a case for Rennie being the inventor of the principle of the ball-race, adding:

> Even if Rennie did not invent ball-bearings, it is quite certain that he was one of the earliest engineers to use them. As fitted by him they consisted of turned castings containing the machined balls in a groove of a larger diameter than that of the spheres concerned, so that true point of contact was obtained between the surfaces.

Cannon balls would have been plentiful at that time and it was quite probably common knowledge that heavy objects, such as guns, could be moved more easily when placed on top of iron balls. The stroke of genius was to take this one step further, by placing the balls in a circular groove to form a ball-race. A ball-race casting can be seen in the Kennet & Avon Canal Trust Museum at Devizes Wharf.

A strap method used to support the two parts of the bridge is shown above at Hilperton Marsh, and an alternative wrought-iron chain above right at Bishops Cannings. The photograph to the right, of Hungerford Church Swing Bridge, illustrates the way a bridge was locked in position by means of a pin and chain. Simple but effective, it would be used probably only when animals were crossing the bridge, or, if it was exceptionally well balanced, to prevent it being blown open by the wind. Bridges of this type were subsequently built for the Lancaster and Rochdale Canals and a modified version appears on the Peak Forest Canal. Rennie was responsible for the construction of the former two canals, but the engineer or contractor of the latter possibly copied Rennie's design. It is conceivable that Edward Barnes, a contractor who carried out various contracts under Rennie's supervision, passed on the ideas of the swing bridge to the Peak Forest Canal Company's Engineer.

On the Kennet & Avon, in 1964, swing bridges had been replaced at two sites by wooden bridges on brick piers at full navigational height, one just east of Hungerford (above) and the other near Foxhangers. Since 1964, some others have been similarly replaced.

Just above the next lock the canal crosses the River Dun by a low, three-arched brick aqueduct. From Hungerford the locks become more frequent, as the canal climbs towards the watershed. Above Froxfield Bridge, water from the Froxfield Feeder enters the canal near the former wharf. The character of the canal changes as it parts company with the River Kennet and heads south-west up the narrow valley of the little River Dun. River, railway, road and canal jostle together for room on the valley floor as, together, they climb up between the rounded hills past Froxfield, the Bedwyns and Crofton. The valley acts as a funnel for gales from the south-west and only the toughest trees survive in the more exposed places in the path of the wind.

Just above Froxfield Upper Lock, No.69, the River Dun passes under the canal via an unusual culvert known as a sump, or siphon, type; that is, where a stream is forced through a U-shaped tunnel underneath the bed of the canal. This is necessary only where the canal needs to cross an existing stream at around the same level. The most impressive example of this kind of culvert used to be at Latton Junction, where the North Wilts Canal forced the fast flowing River Churn to pass underneath, before its junction with the Thames and Severn Canal. There are a few other examples of this type on the Kennet & Avon, but this one near Froxfield is the largest.

Immediately beyond Mill Bridge, which carries the Great Bedwyn to Wilton road, is an unusual cottage between the road and the railway, built of local flints and Bath stone with a slate roof. It was built by a member of the Lloyd family, master masons since the 18th century, and was still owned by a direct descendant in 1964. He told me that the actual design was copied from a mason's 'do-it-yourself' manual, except for the roof, for which there was apparently not enough capital available to complete it in accordance with the design. However, his ancestors (Ben Lloyd and his son John) made a good job of it, as it still stands firm today, despite the effects of diesel expresses thundering past a few yards away. The two Lloyds were not only concerned with the building of Bruce Tunnel and most of the other canal works in the area, but were at one time under contract to the Canal Company to maintain the canal in working order between Brimslade and Reading. Not far from Mill Bridge was the stone which marked the half-way mark, for administrative purposes, of the canal between Reading and Bath. The western section was covered by the maintenance depot at Devizes and the eastern one by that at Newbury Wharf. This stone was moved, subsequently, to a position a little to the west of the Lloyds' cottage. Six years after the canal was bought by the GWR in 1852, John Lloyd's contract ceased and maintenance was carried out by railway employees. The Railway Company continued to use the boundary stone to divide their own regions into east and west of Great Bedwyn, but it has now disappeared.

Mill Bridge at Great Bedwyn is unusual in that it is a skew bridge, that is it crosses the canal at an angle. Cyril Boucher, in his book on John Rennie, goes to some pains to prove that Rennie was the first engineer to experiment with this novel design. This bridge, completed in 1796, was the first of its kind according to Boucher. He illustrates his point with a sketch (opposite) which he says "represents an incomplete application of the principle, for only those portions acute to the face are built with skew courses and these are tailed out to become parallel to the abutments". Up until this time, all bridges had been built at right angles to the natural obstacle, since building at an angle caused the arch to shear along the joint line between the bricks or stone blocks. But it will be apparent from a quick study of the underside of Mill Bridge that here is a compromise and not a proper skew arch at all – the whole thing is a mess.

There is a larger skew bridge next to Burbage Wharf, but this is merely a better version of Mill Bridge. However, about half-way between Locks 62 and 63, there is a purpose-built skew bridge with four separate arch rings of half-brick thickness, each following a different line and thus providing a laminated arch of great strength. As shown in the photographs opposite, the brick courses continue throughout the width of the arch from one springing line to the other. There seems no reason for a skew bridge to have been built here as it only provided access to one field for a single farm. The arrangement of the parapet is slightly different from a standard brick bridge in that it continues upwards at the string course on the same line. It may be, therefore, that this bridge was built by Rennie at a later date as an experiment in building a proper skew arch. Rennie went on to construct skew bridges in both brick and stone; once the principle had been established and seen to work in practice, it was copied by others, notably various railway engineers, but the most extreme example of a canal skew bridge can be seen at Monkhide, seven miles east of Hereford on the Herefordshire and Gloucestershire Canal.

The bridge illustrated here was, strangely, missing from the Ordnance Survey 1" map issued in 1942, although somebody knew it existed as anti-tank blocks were placed on its roadway – they are still there today, like the hump on the old man's shoulders in the fairy story. Incidentally, this map shows all locks east of Crofton pointing downhill (to confuse an invader?). It is gratifying to note that by the time the Landranger 1:50,000 series of maps came out, the bridge had been reinstated and the locks were now facing the correct way.

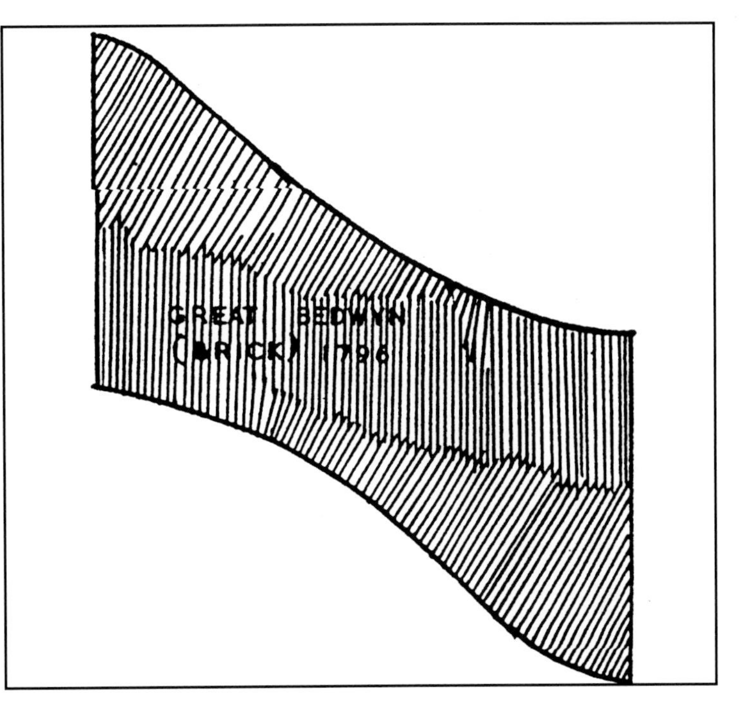
GREAT BEDWYN
(BRICK) 1796

The steady climb up the River Dun valley culminates in the Crofton flight of locks to reach the summit level. Between locks 60 and 61(above), the pound was made extra deep, as water is drawn from it by Crofton Pumping Station. This deepened pound is in turn fed by Wilton Water via a short leat under the towpath (to the left of the lock, following the line of fencing). A tributary of the Dun has been dammed to form a lake (top right), which is supplemented by natural springs and, as originally constructed, could contain 6.9 million gallons of water, but years of silting have reduced this amount to about 4.6 million gallons, according to A. P. I. Cotterell & Sons in 1959, or 140 locksfull of water. The outlet from Wilton Water is approximately four feet below the top of the overflow weirs and is controlled by sluices (bottom right), which permit water to enter a small square settling chamber. On the canal side of this chamber, water flows into the canal and so to Crofton Pumping Station, while on the downstream side the excess water flows on down the valley, following its original course to join the Kennet at Hungerford. Immediately beyond the square chamber are two semi-circular culvert entrances, the far one being set back and at an angle to its neighbour.

As to the pumping station, Ian Bradley states, in his article *The Crofton Beam Engines*, that the original intention was to drive a tunnel some three miles long from about the position of the present pumping station towards Wootton Rivers. He was referring to a map of the projected waterway (on display at the K&ACT Museum at Devizes), which seems quite feasible considering the difficulties in providing an adequate water supply to the summit level. This was of great concern to the committee, because the summit passes through chalk downland where water sources are notoriously scarce. However, the committee decided against the long tunnel, mainly because of the much higher cost involved, but also because of a guaranteed supply of water from near the village of Wilton not far away. Because of an unusual geological formation here, there are many freshwater springs, which were well-known to the Romans – one of their many roads passes close by. These springs feed the aforementioned Wilton Water and, except in times of drought, normally keep it full.

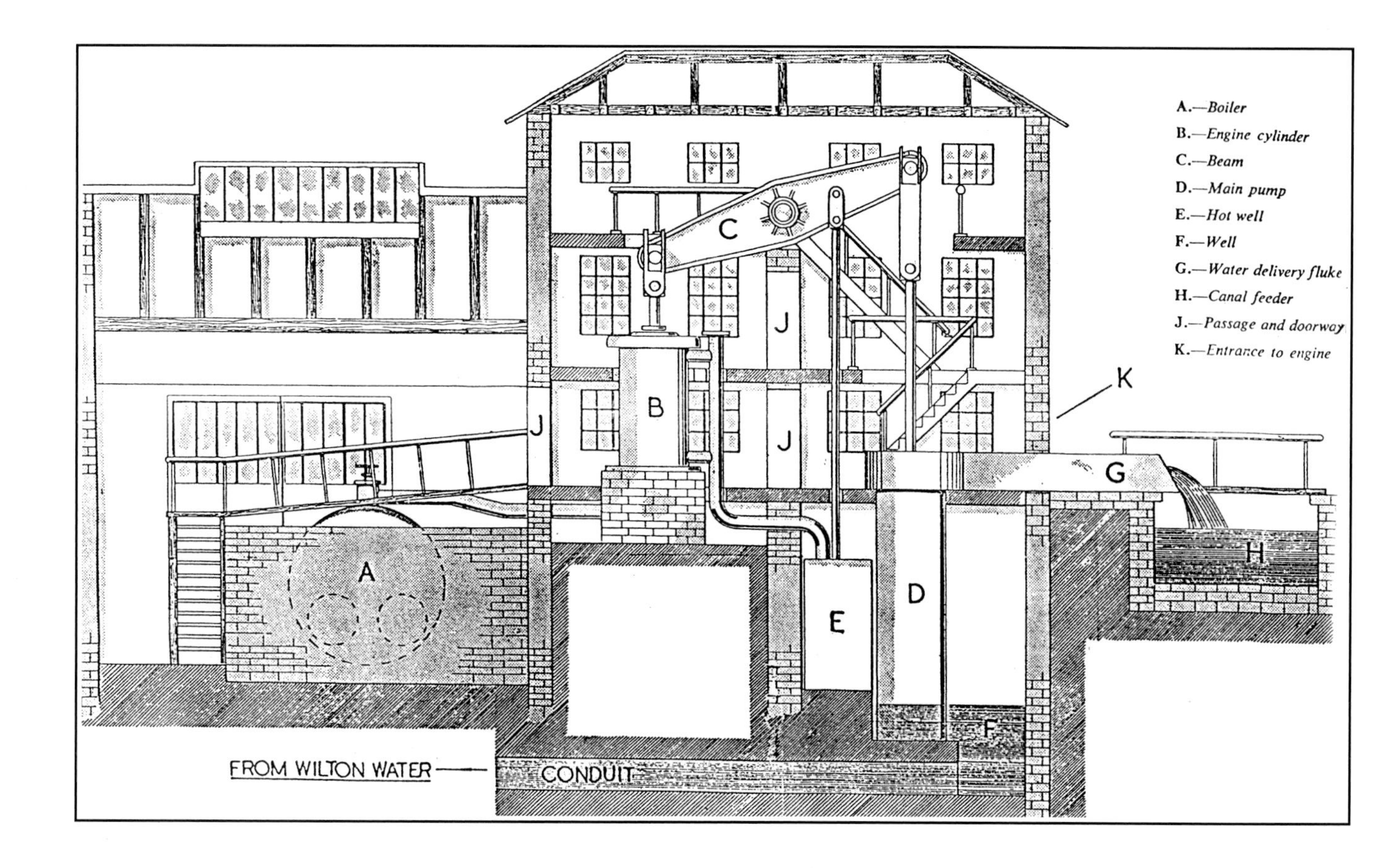

There are several versions of the history of the two beam pumping engines at Crofton. C. P. Weaver of the Railway & Canal Historical Society has supplied perhaps the most accurate of these. He is doubly qualified in that not only has he searched the records, but, as an engineer, he once tended the pumps! The older, or No.1 engine, was built in 1801, originally for the West India Dock Company, but was never used by them and was sold to the K&A the following year. In 1803 it was stored at Froxfield, pending a decision on a site for the pumphouse. Building began in 1807 on the present site and was completed in the following year. Rennie then discovered to his surprise that there was no boiler included in the purchase price for the engine, so he ordered two from Boulton & Watt immediately! As originally constructed, the building housed only the engine, with the steam boiler being out in the open – inspection of the building today will reveal that it has had the boiler room added on. Pumping commenced on 5th November, 1809. On Rennie's recommendation, a second engine was ordered from Boulton & Watt in December of that year, which came into operation early in 1812.

The first chimney stack, made of brick, became unsafe in September 1849. It was demolished and replaced with an iron one, which itself was declared unsafe in 1856, to be replaced by another brick chimney on the present site, in the summer of 1856. The top 30 feet were declared unsafe in 1959 and subsequently removed. The lack of height provided insufficient updraught for the boilers, effectively bringing to an end the operation of the pumps. However, in 1996 the K&ACT launched a Crofton Chimney Appeal to restore the chimney to its original height. This was achieved at the end of April 1997.

In July 1842, Thomas Blackwell, the Crofton engineer, pronounced the old No.1 engine unsafe to work, so a replacement was purchased from H. Harvey & Sons of Hayle, Cornwall, which arrived in late 1846. At the same time the existing wagon-top boilers were replaced with three single-flue Cornish ones. The Boulton and Watt parallel motion was recycled for use with the new engine, the remains of the old one being sold to Harveys for £490. The new Sims No.1 engine began working in 1847. After the GWR took over the Canal Company, the boilers were replaced by Lancashire type ones, made at the GWR's Swindon Works, and installed in 1892 and 1903, which are the ones in use today. The pumphouse is built in brick, with a slate roof supported by a timber framework. The boiler room is of similar construction and is attached to the main building on the canal side. The chimney is connected to the boilers via an underground flue. An underground conduit, or tunnel, brings water to the base of the two pumps, which then each raise a ton of water up 40 feet. This water is discharged into a leat on the uphill side of the pumphouse, where it flows by gravity to the summit pound, which it enters just above Lock No.55. The pumps were in regular use until 1952 and the No.1 engine was last steamed in 1958. Ten years later The Crofton Society started the work of restoration, water being pumped once more only two years later, in 1970. Further extensive work was needed, however, the full story being told in booklets compiled by members of the Society. The engines are 'in steam' on several weekends throughout the year and the whole site is well worth a visit.

A mile or so beyond Crofton Top Lock, the canal passes through Bruce Tunnel. At 502 yards long, this has the largest bore of any canal tunnel in Britain, except Netherton Tunnel on the Birmingham canal system. Begun in 1805, it was completed by July 1809. The two portals are virtually identical; built entirely of red brick, capped with Bath stone, they both have large plaques of Bristol pennant stone, supported by two simple corbels on each side. The plaque on the west end is blank, but that on the east end has an inscription in elegant Roman lettering which reads:

The Kennet and Avon Canal Company
Inscribe this TUNNEL with the Name of
BRUCE
In Testimony of the Gratitude
for the uniform and effectual Support of
The Right Honourable THOMAS BRUCE EARL of AILESBURY
and CHARLES LORD BRUCE his Son
through the whole Progress of this great National Work
by which a direct communication by Water was opened
between the cities of LONDON and BRISTOL
ANNO DOMINI 1810

The tunnel was provided with a chain along the wall on the southern side to enable boatmen to haul their craft through. Although there is no sign of the chain from the entrance, H.A.C.Langford confirmed that it was still there when he passed through, in a letter to the Editor of *The Butty* (the K&ACT's journal) in April 1965. The tunnel passes under the site of Savernake Low Level Station (now demolished), and the main line to the West of England is close to the eastern portal. Emerging from the tunnel, the canal passes through another deep, but longer, cutting of about half a mile, before reaching Burbage Bridge and the A346. This is a massive brick structure, built on the skew and higher than usual to enable the main road to cross the cutting on the level.

Immediately beyond the bridge on the right is Burbage Wharf (above). The former warehouse has been converted into a private residence, though the loading hatches remain visible. The original wharf crane became unsafe and was dismantled in 1971, to be replaced in 1979 by the present replica, made by Stothert & Pitt, Ltd, engineers from Bath.

At Wootton Rivers there is a flight of four locks down to the 15-mile pound. Alongside the Top Lock, No.54, is a cottage which is probably original and has remained largely unaltered, the windows bearing a strong resemblance to those of the mason's cottage at Great Bedwyn (see page 29). There is a two-storey cottage near the bottom lock of the flight, which is also probably original, though disguised by a new tiled roof and chimney stacks.

Rennie's bridges follow a standard design, which was altered slightly to meet local conditions, usually by raising or altering the parapet when the canal passed through a cutting. Similarly, when a bridge was placed immediately below a lock at the lock tail, the arch was flattened somewhat and the lock walls continued to form the base of the arch, as shown illustrated at Wootton Rivers. Similar arrangements appear on early James Brindley canals such as the Trent & Mersey, the Staffs & Worcester and the Oxford Canals, but it is surprising that on a canal built comparatively late in the Canal Age more boatman-friendly bridges couldn't have been built, like those on the Birmingham Canal Navigations and the Worcester & Birmingham Canal.

Having descended from the heights of Savernake Forest, the canal now travels the length of the Vale of Pewsey without a single lock, crossing the course of the Wiltshire Avon, to Devizes. After Wootton Rivers there are some sizeable embankments, between Milkhouse Water and Pain's Bridge, the streams they cross being piped through brick-lined culverts. There are many of these along the canal, for carrying the waters of small streams safely away, in cases where they cannot usefully be fed into it. The standard brick type, as shown above, carries a small stream under a high embankment near New Mill and is typical of many on the canal east of Devizes. The actual tunnel is at least three brick courses thick and each entrance is marked by a brick wall, curved for strength and capped with cement or stone. Those of us who are not bricklayers might like to exercise our brains, by working out how a round tube of about a foot inside diameter and several yards in length, made up of three layers of rectangular bricks, was constructed. The length of the tube would have to be calculated by knowing the height of the completed embankment, the width of canal and the angle of slope of the embankment's sides. A trench would have to be dug alongside the existing stream and the tube constructed in it so that, when completed, the stream could be diverted through it. Only then could building of the embankment begin.

There is one long building at Pewsey Wharf, the end furthest from the canal having been the residence of the wharfinger and the remainder used to store goods that had arrived or were to be sent by canal. It is now leased by the K&ACT.

Canals often passed through large estates and, to appease the lord of the manor, bridges were decorated or built to a particular individual design. A typical example is the castellated footbridge at Drayton Manor Park on the Birmingham and Fazeley Canal, which is purely decorative, as a perfectly good swing bridge exists a few yards away. The vast majority of bridges on the Kennet & Avon Canal are completely devoid of unnecessary decoration, but near Wilcot are found the only three examples of decorated bridges, apart from those in Sydney Gardens in Bath. The first, Bristow Bridge above, just east of Wilcot, is a modest variant of the standard brick design, with recessed panels in the parapet.

The second connects the two parts of Stowell Park and is the only suspension bridge to cross the canal. This bridge was in a rusty, neglected condition and in 1964 had been rendered impassable by the removal of some of the wooden decking, part of which can be seen (above) below the name "Dredge Patentee Bath" cast in the suspension post cross-member. The decking has now been replaced. The bridge was erected at the private expense of Colonel Wroughton of Wilcot in 1845 and is one of only two remaining suspension bridges of this type left in England of some 50 constructed to the design of James Dredge, the other being Victoria Bridge in Bath.

The bridge was erected to allow ample clearance for horse-drawn canal boats passing beneath and this has necessitated the addition of steps at both ends of the structure. Most suspension bridges of that era built by Brown, Telford and Brunel consisted of lengths of chain over support towers, from which vertical cables were hung, to the ends of which was attached the deck (well-known examples being the Menai Straits Bridge and Clifton Suspension Bridge). Wrought-iron eye-bar chain rods were bolted together like a multi-layered bicycle chain. The use of cables to support the bridge meant that it was susceptible to movement in high winds, as the builders of the Menai Straits Bridge soon discovered. Dredge's patent was an improvement on established practice in that at the join of every link of the chain, two long inclined links or hangers would not only support the deck but resist its twisting in high winds by inducing compression. The number of links became fewer as the chain approached the centre, his 'taper principle', leaving a single bar at mid span. In effect, each half of the bridge was cantilevered out from its tower, making it stronger, lighter and cheaper (having less links of expensive wrought-iron chain).

The third bridge is the most decorated of any structure met so far. As can be seen from the illustrations above and right, the amount of decoration is quite remarkable, the more surprising since the track which crosses it leads to open fields and it can be reached only by a service road from a nearby farm. It was built to appease the aesthetic sensibility of Lady Susannah Wroughton of Wilcot Manor; for the same reason the canal was widened to the east of this bridge to give the appearance of an ornamental lake, and known as Wilcot Wide Water. There are several signatures scratched on the bridge, one of which can be seen above the crudely carved draped swag, dated 1881 (below right). It is interesting to note that some of our forebears were just as thoughtless in their defacing of structures as some of our present generation. Lady's Bridge remains in good condition, though two balusters were missing on the south-west side in 1964 (since replaced) and the coping is damaged on the east side. At towpath level the voussoirs (or arch stones) were formerly protected by a roller, but now only the bracket remains. This was either added as a result of grooves being cut into the soft stone, to save the arch from further damage, or else the roller has been missing for many years and the towing grooves have been worn subsequently and later plugged with cement. Some more scratched inscriptions can be seen in this picture (top far right). In the centre of the parapet is a similar draped swag with the inscription: Erected 1808.

Skirting Woodborough Hill, the canal crosses a tributary of the Avon by an embankment and very shortly afterwards arrives at the delightfully named Honeystreet Wharf. Many of the barges which traded on the canal were built and launched at the former boatbuilder's yard here. The boatbuilder was the firm of Robbins, Lane & Pinnegar, timber merchants, who were also canal carriers until c.1933. They built many of the barges and narrow boats used on the K&A, Basingstoke Canal and the Wey Navigation. The firm closed c.1950. A carved stone high on the east face of a chimney shaft on the wharf gave its history in brief: "This wharf commenced 1811. K&A road made 1842. Part of Wharf burnt 1854. Rebuilt and enlarged 1855. This chimney erected 1859." John Gould was instrumental in salvaging the clock when the tower eventually disintegrated in the late sixties. He and the late Denys Hutchings (Hon. Secretary of the K&ACA and the K&ACT for more than 20 years) ensured that the mechanism was restored to working order. It can be seen in its new home at Crofton Pumping Station, mounted in a case designed and made by Roger Hardy. To the right of the bush in the centre of the picture can be seen the wooden post which is all that remains of the wharf's crane; a complete (and larger) version of this can be seen at Burbage Wharf.

Also at Honeystreet is a solidly built structure known as the *Barge Inn*. Built in 1810 and originally known as *The George*, it was burnt down in 1858, but rebuilt in just six months, such was its importance. Being roughly halfway along the canal, it was a major provisioning point for the commercial traffic, functioning as a bakehouse, slaughterhouse, smoke house, cart shed and provider of general foodstuffs, as well as a pub. Its earlier lantern roof has sadly disappeared.

After Honeystreet, the canal crosses a couple of small tributaries of the River Avon and passes the villages of Stanton St Bernard, All Cannings and Allington, with the smooth slopes of chalk downland always in view to the north. The White Horse on Milk Hill, cut in 1812, can be seen from the towpath soon after leaving the *Barge Inn* and remains in sight for several miles. In the picture of Stanton Bridge above left, the simple but effective design of Rennie's bridges can be seen clearly. The main courses of bricks are laid horizontally to give a solid, down-to-earth effect; the line of the roadway is indicated by a brick course, which is continued on the brick buttresses on either side of the bridge, which successfully mark the beginning and end of the structure. The parapet top and buttresses are capped with a round coping, usually of stone, sometimes rounded bricks, which acts as weather protection. The intrados, or underside, of the arch is emphasized by bricks laid at right-angles to the line of the arch. Sometimes the base of the arch is protected from damage by towing lines by the insertion of stone voussoirs, as can be seen above right. The approach walls are capped with stone and help to guide boats towards the centre of the arch; they also prevent erosion of the bank at the base of the arch and serve to emphasize the springing line of the arch.

Skirting the village of Horton, the canal crosses another tributary of the Hampshire Avon by a long embankment, the stream passing through a U-shaped culvert. By-passing Bishop's Cannings to the right, the canal arrives at the *Bridge Inn*, and passes under the other end of the road from Horton.

Then follows a pastoral stretch between open meadowland, with the roar of traffic on the A361 ahead indicating that Devizes is not far away. Devizes has long been an army base and entering the outskirts of the town the canal passes between barracks and store depots, but little is seen of these as the canal retires into a leafy cutting for the last mile before the centre of the town is reached. Making a somewhat dramatic right-angle turn under the A361 at London Road Bridge, the canal emerges into public gaze once more, for the last part of this 15-mile lock-free pound. This bridge is, incidentally, the first of the stone bridges to be met on this half of the canal (apart from Lady's Bridge), since leaving Newbury. West of Devizes the bridges are predominantly of Bath stone. The ravages of time and weather have, however, caused the stone to crumble away and in many cases the bridges have been patched with red and blue brick producing a mottled, blotchy effect, sufficiently marring the beauty of these bridges to make any stonemason worth his salt turn in his grave! In some cases it is hard to tell whether the bridge was built originally of brick, or whether it has merely been extensively patched, as in the photograph of Cemetery Bridge. Bath stone needs to mature and dry out properly, before being cut and laid in the same disposition as it was quarried, or it crumbles.

The canal having passed Roundway Park on the right, a housing estate on the left, and under two more bridges, Devizes Wharf opens out on the left. In 1964 stables had been converted into garages and the wharf area was used as a car park. An ugly collection of corrugated iron shacks lined the waterfront with their backs to the waterway. The cargo loading doors onto the canal of the warehouse had been bricked up and the building used as a garage. Things have changed since then and the whole wharf area has been transformed, with craft centres, etc. Two of the original buildings remain; one has been converted into a theatre and the other, a granary dating from c.1910, is now the K&ACT Museum and Shop. A large public car park is overlooked by new housing and a trip boat operates from the rejuvenated wharf.

Shortly afterwards the top lock of the Devizes flight of 29 locks appears. Over the lock tail is a remarkably fine stone bridge (opposite top), which carries the main road westwards from the town centre. It is an elegant work of plain ashlar masonry with voussoirs and a single keystone joining the arches to the string course, which indicates the level of the roadway. A simple buttress divides the bridge proper from the towpath tunnel (right). From Devizes Top Lock, No.50, as far as Lower Foxhangers, the bridges have a separate towpath tunnel (see opposite below), which originally accommodated a horse-drawn tramroad. This was used while the great flight was under construction, which was not completed until 1810. The tunnel entrance is here embellished with protective stone voussoirs at the base of a flattened arch with a keystone; also an iron plate has been inserted to give protection against damage from towlines. Boatmen must have cursed the lack of a towpath under this type of bridge, as they would have had to cast off and then re-attach their towlines each time they passed through. Near the lock on the south side is an elegant house built in a similar style to that of the bridge, even to the extent of having a string course running round the building immediately below the first floor windows. The eaves are supported by paired, carved, wooden corbels, one pair on either side above each window, and also at the corners of the roof. Immediately below the bridge is a former toll house, built very much in the style of the bridge, but probably pre-dating the latter.

After Devizes Top Lock, No.50, three locks come close upon each other, before the A361 road crosses the canal at Prison Bridge. This is a curved brick structure, with a separate tunnel for the towpath, as with all others on this flight. Prison Bridge (called locally Prisoners' Bridge) is named after the nearby Devizes Prison, now demolished, and has no apparent connection with the story that French prisoners of war were used in the construction of the Caen Hill flight. The original brick parapet, having been demolished too many times by careless vehicles, has been replaced by railings. A stone tablet set into the western face, reads:

This tablet is erected
by the Kennet & Avon Canal Company
to the memory of
JOHN BLACKWELL
who during thirty four years
superintended the works of the Canal
as their Engineer
with fidelity, vigilance & ability.
1840

It is said that when the Company wanted to erect this tablet they asked his widow where she would like it to be placed. She mentioned that he had always regarded the Caen Hill flight of locks as his greatest achievement and so its present position near the head of the flight would be suitable. However, this must have been difficult for her to do as, according to a memorial tablet in Hungerford Church, she had died six months earlier! The bridge is interesting in that it had a matching archway on the opposite side to the towpath tunnel, which has since been bricked up. This was possibly used as a storage place, as the towpath lies on the other side of the canal.

Another two locks and the top lock of the Caen Hill flight is reached, the total fall of the 29 locks being approximately 237 feet. The pounds between Locks Nos. 50 and 44 have been made extra wide and deep to store as much water as possible. Alongside Lock No.44 is the main British Waterways maintenance depot for the whole canal. Here, 16 locks descend in a straight line, providing a most impressive sight, which in 1964 was a scene of neglect and decay. The whole of this section had been allowed to dry out and Nature systematically took over the works of Man. L.T.C.Rolt in his book, *The Inland Waterways of England*, says that, as built, "the capacity of the intervening pounds was increased by extending them laterally so that they form what can best be described as a series of water terraces down the slope". These lateral pounds were not as deep as the main canal, but without them there would have been a real possibility, through gate leakage, of insufficient water being available to fill the next lock down. This would have required water to be run down from a higher pound, which would then itself be short of water, and so on, resulting in a laborious and time-wasting process. Each side pond, as built, held enough water to fill a lock 14 times. All the locks in the flight are of brick, with stone used as a protective capping to the approach and lock walls, and anywhere else extra strength is required, such as the gate quoins and the ground paddle culverts. In 1969 the flight was saved from further destruction by the removal of the wilderness of vegetation by the former Junior Division of the K&ACT. During recent restoration, a footbridge was installed over the tail of each lock, making working through much easier than before. Water supply was always a problem on this flight, which has at last been solved by means of back-pumping the lockage water from the bottom of the flight to the pound above Lock No.44. Beside this lock is an attractive cottage of a design unusual on the canal. Most recently occupied by a British Waterways employee, it was originally the home of the Superintendent Engineer. Later in its life it became a laundry, waste water being discharged into the pound below the bridge, which the boatmen christened Soapy Pound because of the mass of soapsuds which accumulated there. It is built of brick with a tiled roof reaching down to the top of the ground-floor windows. A tiled porch leads to the front door, and access to the towpath side of the canal is provided by a fixed footbridge over the lock tail. From 1829 until 1843 the flight was lit by gas, as reported in the Minute Book of the Canal Company for 18th October 1829:

> The Gas Works along the line of locks at Devizes being now in operation – Resolved that no Barge or Boat be allowed to enter any one of the Devizes Locks after the Gas shall be lighted but on payment of one shilling for each Barge and sixpence for each Boat which payment shall entitle the Owner to navigate his Barge or Boat through the said locks so long as the Gas shall be lighted but not longer.

Clearly both barges and narrow boats were trading regularly on the canal.

Alongside both Lock No.43 (above) and No.29 there used to be a small wooden hut with a tiled roof and a chimney, for use by the lock-keepers on duty. These have long since collapsed. Below Lock No.28 is another of the bridges on this flight of the same design as Prison Bridge. This one is slightly different in that the towpath tunnel has stone courses up to the springing line of the arch; the rest of the structure, including the main arch, is of brick with stone protective coping. Below Lock No.22 is the last of the bridges of this type. In 1964, the main arch showed signs of cracking under the unexpected weight of several concrete tank obstructions and the parapets had been replaced by new iron railings set in concrete, possibly to reduce the weight on the bridge. The obstructions have now been removed and the parapets restored to brick. The towpath crosses to the northern bank once more at this bridge.

Rounding a corner and passing along a straight embankment, the canal crosses the Summerham Brook, the feeder from which enters the canal shortly afterwards. West of Devizes the culverts tend to be of stone – or at least the entrances are – the one for the Summerham Brook being a good example. It will be noticed that the keystone lacks the two flanking stones present on the standard bridges – a mark of social distinction perhaps? This single elongated keystone is a feature of all the stone culverts and lesser arches on the canal.

By far the largest volume of water supplied to the canal direct from a stream is from the Summerham Brook, otherwise known as the Seend Feeder. The course of the stream has been interrupted at a point roughly half-way between the villages of Seend and Rowde, about half a mile to the north of the canal. A leat (to the middle right of the picture) conveys water from here to the canal, the quantity being controlled by special sluices. These are designed to allow flood water from the brook to overflow them in times of flood, while still retaining a head of water in the leat.

Around the next corner the canal passes Martinslade Wharf, now overgrown and with the warehouse converted to a private residence. The actual warehouse, of brick with a tiled roof, has decorative stone quoins set into the corners. At some later date a stone cottage was added to the western end and the two are now one house. At Seend there is a flight of five locks. Near the top lock is a stone lock-keeper's cottage with a tiled roof, still inhabited and consequently in good condition. Between this lock and the third lock can be seen the remains of Seend quarry and ironworks, the latter demolished in 1889, though the ironstone quarry continued to be mined until 1946.The site is now no more than a collection of grassy mounds and hollows. Below Seend Bridge is Seend Wharf (above), now converted for private use. The old stone warehouse is now *The Barge Inn* and the wharf area is used as its car park. The former stables have once again been converted into garages to serve the horses of today. The lengthman's cottage immediately beyond is also of stone with a tiled roof, now a private house with frontage direct onto the canal.

The canal descends two more locks to the valley of the Semington Brook, a tributary of the Bristol Avon. The canal here is straight and less interesting, with only four swing bridges to break the monotony, before reaching the two locks near the village of Semington. Alongside the second, or Semington Bottom Lock, No.15, is a stone cottage with a tiled roof. This makes use of the same decorative device as does the house near Devizes Top Lock, a stone string course round the house at a level in line with the sills of the first floor windows. This form of decoration is used also on the house at Semington Wharf. In 1964 the condition of the lock was comparatively good and there were even handrails on the gate beams, a sight not seen since leaving Cobblers Lock, No.72, only a mile from Hungerford! A small footbridge crosses the lock tail, providing access to the cottage from the towpath. Below the lock, the Wilts and Berks Canal once joined the K&A at this point. Built as a narrow canal and opened in 1810 with 42 locks, it was 51 miles long and ran to the Thames at Abingdon. It was abandoned in 1914 and large sections subsequently filled in. However, there are moves afoot to restore at least parts of it, and the Wilts and Berks Canal Trust has been formed with that aim.

At Semington the bridge over the entrance has been removed and the canal entrance filled in and concreted over. The lock chamber immediately beyond the former bridge has been covered over and is now a cesspool (which restorers should have fun clearing out!) for the attractive stone house (above), where canal tolls were once collected. The handrails over the site of the former entrance bridge are recycled fish-bellied railway lines, which most likely came from the horse-drawn Avon and Gloucestershire Railway when that line was closed in 1906. The railway was acquired, with the K&A, by the GWR in 1852.

Semington Wharf lies immediately beyond the bridge carrying the Melksham to Trowbridge road. The occupants of the house have converted the wharf into a garden which has not, nevertheless, disguised the wharf's original function.

Soon afterwards, the Semington Brook is crossed by a stone aqueduct near the village of the same name. It is a workmanlike structure, though hardly graceful. It carries the canal at full width, with room to spare for paths on both sides, which used to be obstructed by anti-tank blocks – the tops can be seen above the parapet in the picture – since removed on the towpath side. It would appear that the best quality Bath stone was used only for the voussoirs and the area next to the arch, as the majority of the rest has rotted away and been replaced with blue brick, a hideous practice. Large stone tablets have been built into both faces of this aqueduct, but neither has been inscribed. The coping has crumbled away in several places, but the ashlar masonry wall along the top remains in excellent condition on both sides of the aqueduct.

Then follow two straight, pastoral miles and five bridges, through peaceful farming land to Marsh Wharf at Hilperton Marsh. This wharf was at one time owned by A. H. & S. Bird, who sold coal from the Somerset collieries for 5½d (2p) per cwt. (unscreened) and 7d (3p) per cwt. (screened) from here in the 1880s. The coal merchant's office was in the stone building on the left of the picture and the stables were in the building on the extreme right. A modern bungalow has been built in the wharf area and the rest of the wharf converted into a garden. A short distance beyond the wharf and Hilperton Bridge is the smaller Hilperton Wharf with a stone lengthman's cottage, still inhabited, fronting the canal.

After half a mile or so, the canal runs along an embankment as the ground falls away, crosses a small stream passing through a culvert beneath. Then comes the Ladydown Aqueduct, which crosses a railway, followed immediately by the River Biss Aqueduct, the canal at this point following a sweeping curve, before resuming its westward course. Here the canal is carried over the Biss at a much higher level than at Semington. Again the stone has weathered badly and has been patched with yellow brick. The arch is emphasized by large stone voussoirs and outlined by a moulded string course. On either side of the arch, buttresses rise from ground level and are continued through the cornice to the parapet, to give a feeling of strength to the arch, a device used by Rennie in many of his larger works. The large cornice is supported by shaped corbels, but on the south side (below opposite) this has deteriorated to such an extent that it has been removed entirely above the arch and the space filled in with yellow brick. The supporting walls must have been made of poor quality stone, as they are almost entirely patched with yellow brick. While this method is no doubt cheap, quick, adaptable and effective, it nevertheless completely ruins the effect of a uniform whole, as envisaged by the architect. Soon afterwards, the Avon passes close by, although 34 feet or so below.

Passing *The Beehive* at Widbrook the canal follows a natural gap in the hills around Bradford-on-Avon, entering the Avon Gorge, to commence the most dramatic part of its course. Since 1964, a new bridge, Underwood's Bridge, has been built across the canal shortly before Bradford Lock, No.14. This latter is the only lock on the whole length between Semington and Widcombe Top Lock in Bath, an amazing feat of engineering in such difficult country. The building in the centre of Bradford Wharf (top, opposite) is not a warehouse, but a workshop for boats in the dry dock (formerly a gauging dock, where boats were weighed for toll purposes) immediately in front of it. Boats entered the dock, stop planks were inserted and the water let out into the canal below. While in dock, the boat and workmen were (and still are) protected from the weather to a certain extent by the projecting canopy. Other buildings in the wharf area, all built of Bath stone, included the ubiquitous stables, an elegant little toll office (demolished in the late 1960s) alongside the lock, a former wharfinger's house and a pub. On the towpath side by the lock is a large stone house which formerly housed a canal employee. It was here, in October 1794, that the first sod of the Kennet & Avon Canal was cut. The lock at Bradford was, until the amalgamation of Locks Nos.8 and 9 in Bath, the deepest on the canal, with a rise of 12 feet 6 inches. Immediately below Bradford Bridge was a stone building in poor condition, fronting onto the road, probably former stables (bottom, opposite). Just past the house shown on the left of the picture, the canal widens out to the former Lower Wharf, at the end of which is a warehouse end-on to the canal, used in 1964 as an ironmonger's showroom and store. Passing the 14th-century Tithe Barn on the right, the canal is suddenly close to the Avon, clinging perilously to the side of the valley, which is particularly narrow at this point while the river flows past, 70 feet below. In fact, in 1802 the whole canal slid bodily into the Avon. Samuel Smiles, in his *Lives of the Engineers*, explains the accident thus, writing that near Bradford:

> the cutting is mostly through open rock, and beyond that through beds of tough clay interspersed with strata of fuller's earth. The water at these points worked serious mischief, for after a heavy fall of rain it would filter through the earth, and the weight of the mass pressing down from above, tended to force out the soft clay, causing extensive slips. On one occasion, not less than seven acres of land slid into the canal, forcing the whole down into the river in the valley below. To remedy this source of mischief, soughs or small tunnels were carried into the hillside for a considerable distance, at a level much below that of the canal.

This mishap was one of the contributory causes of the final cost of the canal considerably exceeding the estimate and has caused trouble on this stretch ever since that time.

Draining the canal for repairs, or to let off unwanted water in an emergency, was done on the bath plug principle. A square, wedge-shaped plug of iron-bound wood (top left, opposite) was withdrawn from the centre of the canal bed, by means of a handspiked winch (top right, opposite). The roller had a ratchet at one end and the chain from the plug was led over a roller, mounted in the stone block in the foreground. The released water ran through a specially built culvert (bottom left, opposite) to a nearby river, in this case the Avon near Bradford. One wonders what happened when the chain broke at the plug end! On the canal section proper, water level between locks was maintained through ground-paddle culverts acting as overflow weirs, as on the Rochdale Canal, which allowed excess water to pass through the lock to a lower level. Nearby streams were utilised for flood relief weirs and numerous examples can be seen along the canal, an elaborate one being seen on page 86. Where there was a high risk of an embankment blowout – which could lead to the loss of millions of gallons of water, not to mention loss of life as well as other damage – single pairs of stop gates were constructed (bottom right, opposite). These had rudimentary sluice gear, but no beams and were designed to close automatically on either side of possible sources of danger, the force of escaping water slamming them shut. These are numerous between Trowbridge and Bath, in many cases sited where the canal narrows at a bridge. On long pounds, where a leak might occur anywhere, double stop gates were installed, that is, two pairs of gates facing in opposite directions. When it was desired to drain the canal for any reason, that section was 'stopped off', by the insertion of specially provided stop planks into stop grooves. These grooves were cut vertically into the walls of most locks at the head and tail, and into both approaches to many of the bridges. A stack of stop planks can be seen in the picture of Lady's Bridge on page 46.

Hurriedly passing a sewage works on the left, where the steep bank opens out a little, the canal passes through a wooded cutting, once again too close for comfort to the Avon flowing below, before turning sharply to the right to cross the aqueduct at Avoncliff. When boats were horse-towed on the canals, sharp corners such as this were something of a problem and towing posts were erected, like the one shown, to save property from damage by the towline. Over the course of years, countless towlines have worn deep grooves in these posts, which stand today as silent memorials to boatmen of past generations who worked, lived and died 'on the cut'. Holes in the post mark the position of wooden plugs, to which was once attached a cast-iron protective plate, or a wooden roller. Whichever it was, it has been missing for many years, as indicated by the presence of such deep grooves.

Between Avoncliff and Dundas the towpath changes sides to the left bank. Westbound boats would have had to stop on the aqueduct while the horse was unhitched, led down past *The Cross Guns*, under the southern arch and back up to the towpath, as there is no bridge at this point. Here, near the hamlet of Avoncliff, the Avon valley narrows considerably and, for engineering reasons, the canal crosses to the north side, where the bank is not quite so precipitous. It is carried by a graceful three-arch aqueduct of Bath stone, approximately 330 feet long, which has weathered somewhat better than the aqueducts mentioned so far, and consequently has received less attention from the repairers. The central, elliptical arch (above, opposite) has a span of 60 feet, and the arches on either side are semi-circular and have spans of 34 feet. The line of the voussoirs is outlined by a plain string course similar to that on the Biss Aqueduct. The courses are of alternate ashlar and rock-faced masonry, though the effect has been spoiled on the faces of the smaller arches, especially on the south side, by brick patching. The cutwaters are continued upwards as splayed buttresses to the parapet (below, opposite), to produce bays off the towpath. This strengthens the parapet and provides psychological support to the central arch.

Despite this, it has sagged quite noticeably, apparently during or soon after construction, as it has lasted like this for many decades without collapsing. The size of the cornice is in proportion to the rest of the structure, and from a distance is emphasized by the plain, squared corbels. The parapet is of plain ashlar masonry with a central stone suitable for the engraving of a dedication. There is also a long, uninscribed tablet above the central arch immediately below the entablature on each face. There is no date on the tablet, but there is every reason for supposing the aqueduct was completed in 1797, from date marks found on the parapet, although the K&A Report to Subscribers, dated 26th June 1798, states that: "The Avon Cliff Aqueduct is finished, except the inverted arch".

The parapet is solid, except for three sets of balusters on the abutments. The abutments have a concave batter, curving inwards and upwards, and are terminated by square buttresses, followed by wing walls with protective coping. Boucher describes the entablature as Corinthian, "not a slavish copy of some Roman original, but a simplified version, Rennie's own design". The aqueduct was re-lined and repaired in 1978 and the length between Dundas and Bradford re-opened to navigation in 1984.

Having crossed to the northern or right bank of the River Avon, the canal has to fight almost as hard for a foothold as it did near Bradford. But the route chosen is the lesser of two evils, as the other bank is even steeper, especially near Limpley Stoke. Two lengthman's cottages are passed before Dundas Aqueduct is reached, both inhabited and in good condition; both are in stone with a tiled roof, but each has a quite different character. This length has been completely rebuilt and lined throughout with concrete, which hopefully, has at long last cured the perennial problems of leakage encountered on this stretch. At the corner immediately after the second cottage, where the canal swings sharp left to cross the aqueduct, are two iron corner posts, the first one being shorter and fatter than its companion. Both are scored with the marks of many towlines, as is the one on the far side of the aqueduct. It is said that these pipes came from Claverton Pumping Station and were used originally to convey water from the pumps up to the canal above. Perhaps they were surplus to requirements, or perhaps they were damaged and therefore unable to be used for their purpose; certainly the one at the wharf end of the aqueduct retains its coupling flange (complete with square bolt holes and lining of pitch) while the flange on its partner has been broken off.

Dundas Aqueduct is by far the most noteworthy work in stone on the canal, so that it was fortunate indeed that by 1964 it had been scheduled for preservation by the Ministry of Works. The central arch, which spans the river, measures 64 feet in diameter and the two oval, or lozenge-shaped arches on either side measure 20 feet in diameter. The central portion of the main arch is straight, both vertically and horizontally, the outward thrust from the waterway and its puddled bed being taken by iron tie bars inserted just below the bed of the canal. The abutment walls, which curve out at each end have a concave batter, as at the other aqueducts, and the structure is terminated by wing walls, which hold up the earthwork of each approach embankment. Boucher describes the aqueduct as "an exercise in the Roman Doric order". The aqueduct is remarkable for the extremely large cornice which juts out about four feet from the faces of the aqueduct (see page 80). As can be seen from the picture above, in 1964 there were several small leaks in the eastern arch and abutment wall, which had stained the walls rather badly. The south face has weathered well and is in good condition, but the north face has been extensively patched with brick, thus losing much of the architectural detail (see page 81).

In the centre of each parapet is a large plain stone block, perhaps for an inscription or merely to accentuate the centre of the structure. Below these blocks and below the cornice on either side are two bronze dedication tablets. That on the south face reads:

TO CHARLES DUNDAS ESQ.
CHAIRMAN OF THE KENNET AND AVON CANAL COMPANY
FROM ITS COMMENCEMENT A.D.M.DCC.XCIIII.
THE PROPRIETORS,
MINDFUL OF HIS IMPORTANT SERVICES,
AND HIS UNREMITTED EXERTIONS
THROUGH A PERIOD OF XL YEARS,
GRATEFULLY INSCRIBE THIS TABLET.
A.D.M. DCCC.XXVIII

The equivalent dedication on the north face of the aqueduct is inscribed:

TO THE MEMORY OF
JOHN THOMAS,
BY WHOSE SKILL, PERSEVERANCE AND INTEGRITY,
THE KENNET AND AVON CANAL
WAS BROUGHT TO A PROSPEROUS COMPLETION,
A.D.M.DCCC.X.
THE PROPRIETORS
GRATEFULLY INSCRIBE THIS TABLET.
A.D.M.DCCC.XXVIII

This refers to Jonathan Thomas, a Quaker and Superintendent of the Works in 1803, who did far more for the canal than he has been given credit for by historians. Although the aqueduct was completed in 1798, these tablets were not fixed until many years later. The date on both plaques is 1828, which is incorrect, as according to the relevant K&A Minute Book, they were not put up until 1838, ten years later. This must have been a tricky job – did they erect scaffolding from the river bed, or did they lower two volunteers from the towpath above?

Having crossed the aqueduct, the entrance to the former Somersetshire Coal Canal, which provided the K&A with one of its main sources of revenue, can be seen to the left. Closure of this canal in 1898 caused the demise of the agricultural Wilts and Berks Canal, although the decline in the coal trade had begun in 1854 when the first railway connection was established with the Mendip coalfield. Similarly, this reduced the income from tolls for the K&A. The first lock of the SCC can be seen in the garden of the house near the junction. This part of the canal was filled in, as was the lock chamber, and the whole completely grassed over, with the exception of the coping stones of the chamber walls, which thus indicated clearly the exact location of the lock for future restorers. The short section from Dundas Wharf to the A36 road bridge was excavated in 1985 and has been restored by Tim Wheeldon of the Bath & Dundas Canal Company; it is now in use as a marina. During excavation of the lock chamber, it was discovered that, although now narrow, it had been converted to broad gauge at some stage, the recesses for wide gates remaining. At the canal's entrance is an aluminium bridge, recycled from the Alcan Works near Banbury on the Oxford Canal. Alongside the wharf at Dundas in 1964 was one of the few remaining examples of the type of barge formerly trading on the canal, unfortunately broken up a few years later.

But there remains a good example of a crane used for loading and unloading cargo. The slewing gear seems to have been damaged (perhaps done deliberately to prevent it being used) and the cable has gone, but otherwise this early example of cast-iron work appears to be in excellent condition. There are also two small stone buildings on the wharf, the first originally a toll office, complete with chimney and list of regulations, the other a simple structure with a pyramid shaped roof, probably used as an equipment store. This second structure (see previous page), curiously has huge doors at both ends, but no windows. It has been set down with no regard to other users – there is barely enough space left for walkers to pass – and its position bears no relation to the rest of the wharf, being at an odd angle to the wharf wall.

Just to the north of the wharf, is the only bridge of its type on the canal. The flat, iron deck of the bridge, which is supported by stone buttresses, is not original, and the balustrade is a steel copy of the original woodwork. It is possible that this was intended to be a cast-iron arch, similar to that found in Sydney Gardens. It is, however, certain that this was not merely a standard bridge which had failed and then been converted to support a cast-iron arch. The presence of protruding buttresses on both sides of the arch and the line of the string course discount that idea. Why Rennie chose to use this form of construction, only further research will reveal. It is just possible that his choice of material was connected in some way with the nearby Claverton Pumping Station.

It is conceivable that this bridge was designed and built with a flat 'arch' to take a tramroad, by which blocks of stone from Conkwell quarry on the other side of the aqueduct could be conveyed to Dundas Wharf. But the fact that this quarry developed its own wharf at the eastern end of the aqueduct, and in any case that the stone was of inferior quality and not used for long, throws doubt on this theory. Also, the approach to the bridge from the towpath is far too steep for a tramroad, nor is there any sign of rails ever having been in place. It is also a turnover bridge, that is where the towpath changes sides. Horses towing boats travelling towards Newbury would need to cross it, the towline would be unhitched and the boat would pass beneath the bridge before turning to cross the aqueduct. The horse would carry on along Dundas Wharf, over the bridge at the entrance to the Somersetshire Coal Canal and onto Dundas Aqueduct, where the boat's line would be re-connected. On the downstream side of the aqueduct, at the eastern end, a stone horse-stile existed until demolished a few years ago. This prevented horses from passing through, while allowing access for pedestrians.

Between Dundas Wharf and Claverton, opposite the towpath, can be seen a classic example of how canal engineers used streams both to supply the canal with water and to act as an overflow channel in time of flood. A stream, known as the Sheepwash Feeder, flows into the chamber by a channel in the foreground of the picture, now overgrown and silted up. The silt is then allowed to settle in the chamber (half filling the chamber in October 1964), and water is let into the canal by means of the sluice and channel to the left. The overflow leaves the chamber to the right, to flow along its original course and pass under the canal through a culvert (top right of picture). This culvert also receives flood water from the canal through two quadrant-shaped apertures, flowing down a series of stone steps before entering the culvert.

At Claverton a pumping station supplied the canal with water extracted from the Avon, using the power of the river itself to work the pump. Two cottages, probably built by the Canal Company to house the men who maintained the station, lie uncomfortably close to the railway, which rudely thrusts its way between them and the building housing the pumping machinery. The machinery is housed in a stone building completed in October 1810, with a tiled roof supported by a wooden framework. It is possible that the roof was made elsewhere and assembled on site, as many joints have Roman numerals carved into them, like a giant d.i.y. kit. The waterwheel is protected by a wooden extension to the main building, which has a stone end wall. Considering the lavish decoration expended on Dundas Aqueduct, it is remarkable that such a vital and innovative piece of machinery should be housed in such a singularly plain structure, completely devoid of decoration. Comparing the photograph above with the drawing (right) will give some idea of the station's layout.

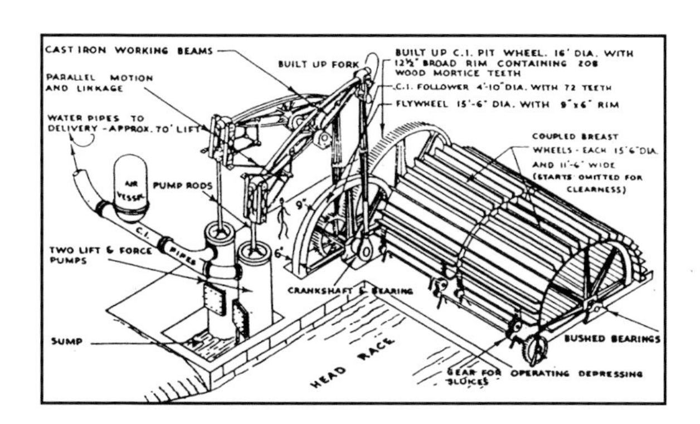

The actual pumping machinery was made in Rennie's London workshops and installed during the following two years. In June 1812 it was minuted that iron pipes, for conveying water up to the canal, from Fox and Co.'s Neath Abbey Ironworks, would be delivered to Bristol. As these would be the last items to complete the installation, it can be assumed that the station commenced pumping by March 1813. Water from a leat off the River Avon was admitted into a settling pond via sluices (above right), which then turned the breast-shot water-wheel (below right), when the so-called depressing sluices were opened.

This huge water-wheel, 24 feet wide and about 19 feet 4 inches in diameter, turned a train of cast-iron wheels (right) which operated two large pumps by means of a crankshaft and two pivoted beams (above). The state of the machinery had been deteriorating for many years when, on 13th November 1952, it is reputed that a log jammed the waterwheel and the sudden deceleration stripped all the oak teeth from the main pit wheel. From then on, water was supplied to the nine-mile pound by means of a diesel-powered pump. Subsequently, the machinery was restored to working order by members of the K&ACT, who in 1984 produced a booklet which lists full details and dimensions, as well as chronicling the account of restoration, which could only be hoped for in 1964. The pumping station is open on Sundays and Bank Holidays between April and October, and can be seen in operation once a month.

After Claverton the valley widens out and the hills have retreated considerably by the time Bathampton is reached. The bridge here is a perfect example of the stonemason's craft and shows what all the bridges on this section of the canal looked like originally, when the stone had been seasoned and laid correctly. Here, the same pattern is followed as in the brick bridges, except that the arch centre is emphasized by a slightly protruding triple keystone. This device appears on bridges on the Lancaster Canal and the Hebden Aqueduct on the Rochdale Canal – Rennie, it will be no surprise to learn, was Engineer to both canals.

The nearby *George Inn* was serving ale long before the canal arrived. The front door faces onto the road, now redirected over the canal by a bridge 50 yards away, access to the towpath being provided via a 'new' door on the first floor. The row of cottages immediately beyond the inn must have been built after the canal, as their doors face onto the towpath and the row is in line with the course of the canal. Approaching Bath, architectural works worthy of note come thick and fast, some being part of the canal as originally designed and some being built to serve the canal, such as toll-houses and warehouses. Along this valleyside section from Bathampton, the Victorian terrace development of the suburbs of Lambridge, Larkhall and Lower Swainswick can be seen across the valley. The canal passes a building fronting onto the towpath, formerly known as Darlington Wharf, just before entering Sydney Gardens. This may have been built by some carrying company as an office, for its design has little in common with other works on the canal, the tops of the windows and doorway being rounded in Norman style. Next to it is a long, low building, once the offices for a regular passenger service between Bath and Bradford run by the horse-drawn 'Scotch' boats, so named because they were wrought-iron boats which had been built in Scotland.

Then the canal dives into a short tunnel and enters Sydney Gardens and the suburb of Bathwick, on the last and most interesting part of its course. Entering the gardens from the north, or Bathampton end, the tunnel entrance is perfectly plain, like any other bridge and gives no hint as to what is to follow. The 165-foot tunnel is of stone throughout, with numerous masons' marks in evidence. Looking back at the tunnel entrance on the south side, the whole façade is elaborately rusticated. The arch line is emphasized by plain dressed voussoirs without a keystone. Above the arch is a large tablet, on which appears an unknown man's head, complete with beard and moustache, draped with a large swag, more elaborately carved than that at Lady's Bridge. Flanking the façade are slightly projecting buttresses of plain dressed stone, which contrast with the rusticated work, each containing a large, empty niche surmounted by a small swag. Above the tablet are three courses of plain dressed stone, the top course containing the corbels, which support a simple moulded projecting cornice. The parapet over the cornice has some blocks missing, but still has the central block which Rennie often used to finish his larger works, such as Avoncliff and Dundas Aqueducts.

Sydney Gardens was a speculative venture promoted by a group of prominent worthies and opened in 1795, following the success of Vauxhall Gardens in London. The proprietors of Sydney Gardens extracted a payment of 2,000 guineas from the Canal Company for permission to pass through their gardens. One of the proprietors was George Stothert, a prominent ironmonger in Bath, who later supplied quantities of ironwork to the Canal Company. Another was Eleazer Pickwick, landlord of the *White Hart* and reputed to be the stagecoach proprietor immortalized in *The Pickwick Papers* by Charles Dickens. The name Pickwick is so unusual that it might be thought he had invented it, but not so. The passage of the canal through Sydney Gardens forms one of the most attractive features of the canal. *The Kennet & Avon Canal – Re-development Scheme* says that "it is clear that the waterway is one of Bath's most valuable amenities, and a great feature of this beautiful public park". The canal is hidden away behind large banks of rhododendrons in a cutting of its own. It would be easy to miss it altogether unless one crossed either of the two footbridges which span the cutting. The peace and quiet of the place is regularly shattered by the whistling, chortling scream of diesel expresses clawing their way up the slope from Bath Spa station. A powerful sound, some would say a beautiful sound, but one which compares ill with crumbling stonework and dead leaves on a deserted canal. It is almost as if the trains shout their derision at a defeated rival as they thunder past, through a cutting of their own a few yards away. But while Rennie's canal is modestly hidden away, Brunel's railway is like a stage setting, the ground sloping gently down towards the lines like an amphitheatre, so that passing trains can be seen and admired against a backdrop of a long stone wall, topped by flowering bushes, as they enter stage right and exit stage left.

After the first tunnel, the canal widens immediately to form a small basin or passing place – purely ornamental, as there can be no reason why working boats would need to stop in a public park, except to allow another boat to pass. It is puzzling that the two cast-iron bridges that follow should be quite so different. If Rennie had designed them, then surely they would have been a matched pair. Hugh Torrens, in his excellent, concise study, *The Evolution of a Family Firm: Stothert and Pitt of Bath*, states that: "These were ordered from the Coalbrookdale Company, the choice being made by the Sydney Gardens Proprietors from designs sent by Coalbrookdale". So, all is made clear, a committee chose the designs from an early mail-order catalogue! Perhaps if these bridges were stock items it might help to explain why they are so small, pinching the canal into three sections. They were certainly modest in scale, but graceful in concept, when compared with other cast-iron structures, which had been built by that time, notably Telford's aqueduct at Longdon-on-Tern. Square-headed bolts fasten together the various sections of each bridge, as close inspection of the underside of each arch will reveal. The two bridges in Sydney Gardens provide access from one part

of the park to another and each has a tablet inscribed "Erected Anno 1800" on both sides, in the centre of each arch. The first bridge has a pronounced skew, crossing the canal at an angle, and may have been provided with protective rollers at towpath level, but these have long since gone. An early signature scratched in the stonework reads "J. Hodges 1869". The spandrels of the first bridge are solid, but are relieved by raised mouldings, which follow the line of the arch. The railings used on this bridge employ an interesting, yet functional diamond pattern, a motif to be found on Lady's Bridge. In the widened section between the two bridges, access to the park is provided via stone steps and an iron gate (not original) through the stone wall, with railings on either side. This has been elegantly done, probably for safety reasons to provide easy access to the towpath.

The second of the two bridges is smaller and more graceful, using only four cast-iron sections, each with a pattern of rings, which give lightness with maximum strength. The marriage of iron with stone seems awkward. An attempt has been made to continue the moulding from iron to stone, but the spandrels seem to have jostled their way between the stone of the abutments at great inconvenience to the walls. The moulded string course on the abutments is unusual in having groups of guttae, rather like prominent front teeth, attached to its lower edge. Originally, this bridge had two bands for protection against towlines, only one of which remains. The balustrades are quite different to those on the first bridge. On the arch they are of simple design, but on the abutments a diagonal cross-pattern appears, the top rail ending with a flourish (right).

After the two cast-iron bridges comes another short tunnel, 175 feet long, with a façade almost identical to that on the first tunnel. The tablet on this one has, however, a female head, much disfigured by decay of the stone after years of exposure to the weather. Purely supposition, but could it be that, as the canal connects two notable rivers, the female head represents Sabrina, or the River Severn and the male head on the other tunnel portal represents Old Father Thames? This portal is in poorer condition than its counterpart, with several blocks from the parapet missing – chips in the cornice indicate where they have gone! Astride the southern portal of this second tunnel is *Cleveland House*, the original headquarters of the Canal Company, a classical piece of Georgian architecture. The stone course connecting the first floor window sills can be seen clearly, a device noted already on other works along the canal. Built by Henry, Duke of Cleveland, probably by local architect John Pinch, it first appeared on town maps as *Canal House* in 1825. It is quite astonishing that a three-storey stone house should have been built on top of a tunnel entrance. Although the side walls do not bear directly down onto the walls of the tunnel, the canal proprietors must have had supreme confidence in the ability of their masons to permit the imposition of this unexpected extra weight. In the roof of this tunnel, approximately 33 feet from the south end, is a rectangular off-centre hole, through which, it is said, messages to boatmen were passed from the Canal Company's offices above. This raises intriguing questions as to what happened if

the boatman missed catching the message – did he have to go round again (Newbury, North Foreland, Land's End, Bristol to Bath)? How did the office know the boatman had caught the message? Or what happened if someone walking through the tunnel intercepted the message before the boatman could get hold of it? Exploration of the cellar revealed that the shaft exists and a hole still enables objects to be dropped to the water below, but the idea that this was done without the messenger being able to see the boat passing beneath beggars belief. More likely is that the shaft continued to the floor above, where some framework existed (any trace of which has now disappeared) allowing messages and/or packages to be transferred by means of a rope or pole. But then the awkward question arises, why bother with a shaft anyway, when a Company clerk had merely to open a window and give any messages to a boat horse boy, as he led his horse along the path over the tunnel entrance, to be passed on to his master? Perhaps it was simply used for verbal messages to passing boats, rather than the written word, as suggested by Valerie Bowyer in her book *Along the Canal in Bath*. Shortly afterwards is Pinche's, or Sydney Wharf, where the water frontage has been altered extensively. However, most of the original warehouse still remains, including a wooden gallery built out over the canal some eight feet or so, which protected cargo while it was being unloaded. The canal widens here to allow for the mooring and turning of boats. This wharf is followed by a bridge, at the top end of Raby Place, remarkable only for the unusual carved design of the parapet. It illustrates clearly the effects of erosion on the faulty part of the Bath stone from which it was cut. Some of the panels have become so bad that they have been replaced in recent years. None of the parapet is original, as part of the string course remains on the east side to show that the bridge was of standard design prior to the road improvement.

Opposite the towpath, just by this bridge, is a large, imposing Georgian house. The familiar architectural features will be recognised but, in addition, the presence of balustrades round the balconies on the first-floor windows are worthy of note. The continuation of the window verticals to the eaves is most unusual and the lintels are decorated. The large number of chimneys bear witness to an earlier age, when coal was the source of heating and servants were two-a-penny. Shortly after this bridge is another wharf with the original warehouse (roofed with asbestos sheeting in 1964); the wharf area is now a garden (above). Not far away is an unusual warehouse fronting the canal opposite the towpath with "Hugh Baird and Sons, Maltsters" still visible on an end wall. The windows are paired and in Norman style, as is the large cargo hatch on the third floor. Then comes the first lock of the Bath flight, Widcombe Top Lock, No.13. Alongside this lock is another toll office, this time with pointed, or Gothic type, arches over its windows and doorway. In 1964 it appeared to be in use as a British Waterways office, judging by the number of notice boards attached to the building.

Below Top Lock, No.13, and Wash House Lock, No.10, on the Widcombe flight are two delightful cast-iron footbridges. With three spandrels each, the ring pattern used is a copy of that used for the larger version in Sydney Gardens. The handrails on these bridges are elaborate, especially on the second one. The first (above) has a simple balustrade of wrought-iron, serviceable and graceful, the uprights held in place by the time-honoured practice of sinking them into holes in the masonry, into which molten lead is poured.

The second bridge (above) is a fine example of the blacksmith's art, but somewhat fussily ornamented with vicious looking arrowheads. As can be seen, the uprights have been braced by horizontal clamps, which have probably saved the structure from further disintegration. Torrens provides convincing proof that both these bridges were cast by Stothert and Pitt and erected after 1815, to provide access for the residents of the newly-built Sydney and Caroline Buildings respectively, across the canal. Before their installation, residents had been obliged to walk across the lock gate beams, a risky business and on one occasion fatal! Alongside Lock No.11, next to the towpath, is a chimney with an unusually ornate decoration near the top, which is all that remains of one of two pumping stations on the flight.

After lock No.11, the canal broadens out to form an ornamental basin, which also acts as a storage reservoir for the rest of the flight. By St Matthew's church the canal turns westward once more for the last few hundred yards before joining the Avon.

Since 1964, the traffic bottleneck at Pulteney Road Bridge has been eased by the building of a new road. The crossing of the canal at low level necessitated the merging of Locks Nos.8 and 9 into one extra-deep lock, now renumbered as 8/9 with a depth of 19 feet 5 inches, which must be quite an experience to pass through on a boat. After this lock, the canal passes under Rossiter Road Bridge, which is a modern replacement for the original Pulteney Road Bridge (above).

The towpath changes sides for the last time here and passes down Ebenezer Terrace in front of Waterloo Buildings (now demolished).

Next to the Bottom Lock, No.7, is the second of the two former pumping stations which supplied water to the canal from the Avon for a short time in the 1830s. However the Avon mill owners objected to the pumping of water from the river and as the K&A Canal Company did not have statutory powers to pump, they had to stop in order to avoid legal action. It is seen here with lock No.8 in the foreground and the former high-level Bath Spa station signalbox on the skyline. Known locally as Thimble Mill, it was not built as a pumping station, but may have been connected with the woollen trade, as suggested by its name. Nothing remains of the pumping machinery and only the shell of the building is left, now part of the adjacent hotel complex. The top of the square chimney has unusual decoration in the form of semi-circular blocks (right). From the bridge leading to Thimble Mill below lock No.7, a broad path leads to the Avon towpath, Bristol and the Sea.

Stone Supplies

Frequent reference has been made already to the poor condition of some of the works in stone and the consequent patching with brick that had been necessary. While the use of brick shows a lack of sensitivity and thought for future generations by the officials of the GWR, it must nevertheless be said in their defence, that the material used originally in the construction of most of the works in stone was often either faulty or incorrectly laid. As mentioned previously, the section from Foxhangers to Devizes was connected by a plate tramroad for the transport of goods while the flight of locks was being built. Stone for the locks may have been delivered on site by this method. The proprietors of the canal seem to have taken it for granted that Bath stone would be used, no doubt because some of them had financial interests in the quarries near Bath. The contractors quarried for stone at Bradford-on-Avon, Monkton Combe, and anywhere else convenient. Plate rails and wagons for the tramroads, to convey the stone to the canal, were brought in from Merthyr Tydfil. Arthur Elton, in his excellent article on *The Pre-History of Railways*, has expertly and eloquently written about the characteristics of Bath stone. On page 39 he describes it as

> a warm, yellow stone, perfectly uniform in colour and of fine texture. It is soft and easy to cut, and is extracted from its beds in large blocks, each usually weighing several tons. These must be stacked to allow the moisture, or "quarry sap", to dry out, when the stone becomes hard and white. On exposure it gradually develops a hard skin, and often weathers to a beautiful honey colour. In winter the blocks are seasoned underground out of reach of frost. In summer they may be seasoned above ground. Though modern methods often enable the blocks to be cut to size at the quarry, in former times it was necessary wherever possible to transport the blocks to the building site and there to cut them to shape as various jobs demanded.

Arthur Elton continues, on pages 54-5:

> Properly selected, quarried, seasoned and laid, Bath stone is a splendid building material, but it is a difficult stone for the inexperienced or the unwary. It is essential to avoid stone which weathers badly or does not stand up to frost; it is necessary to select particular qualities of stone for particular purposes; once selected, the stone must be properly seasoned; it must be laid in the position it occupied in the original bed or it will crumple up like a book turned on end and pressed down.
>
> These rules seem to have been neglected in the building of the Kennet and Avon, with disastrous results to the masonry. By the middle of 1801, the situation had got so bad that the proprietors decided to open their own quarry at Conkwell, on the brow of the hill on the Wiltshire side of Dundas Aqueduct. A steep, double self-acting railway incline about 700 yards long with an average gradient of about 1 in 5 was put in to lower the stone to the canal below. Nattes described it in his book on Bath, published in 1806. "Immediately above one end of ... [Dundas Aqueduct] ... "– he wrote – "is an inclined plane for the purpose of bringing down stone etc. from the neighbouring hill: as the full waggons descend, the empty ones are drawn up by means of a connecting chain [actually a rope]. The accumulated velocity of the descending loaded ones is retarded and regulated by a friction wheel at the commencement of the plane."
>
> Why Conkwell was selected is a mystery, for the stone there was as defective as anything dug by the contractors, and it was abandoned in a short time. Even if Ralph Allen's old quarries on Combe Down were worked out, and this is not certain, there were supplies of stone on Claverton Down and Bathampton Down. Perhaps the canal proprietors could not agree a price with the quarry-owners. Whatever the reason, by March 1802 negotiations had been started with a Mr. Stafford Smith for stone on Claverton Down. James Mills, one of the agents of the canal, who was subsequently dismissed for financial peculation, was instructed to survey the ground for a rail road, "from Claverton Down Quarry to the line of lockage." This line does not appear to have been laid. Instead a mile-long inclined plane was built from Bathampton Down to a point on the canal near Holcombe Farm, at a gradient of about 1 in 5. It features in the first Ordnance Survey of 1808-9 and may well date back to 1802.

The opening of the Bathampton Down incline came, however, too late to save the Canal Company from a great deal of extra expense resulting from the effects of faulty stone and bad masonry. In March 1803, Rennie suggested that the proprietors should cut their losses and use brick instead, as brick-making clay was plentiful in the area around Devizes. But the proprietors stuck to stone and even opened a further quarry at Murhill, near Winsley, between Avoncliff and Limpley Stoke, in 1803. Two years later Rennie reported that the cost of completing the western section between Seend and Bath would be over £87,000. Though he gave several reasons for this vast increase to his original estimate, including the rise in the cost of labour, the principal explanation came down to the bad quality of the stone used. More than two years later again, in June 1807, Rennie was still advising the proprietors to use brick, but with no success, with the results that we can see today. The positions of the three inclined planes which were used for transporting stone blocks from the hillside quarries to the canal side are shown on the map.

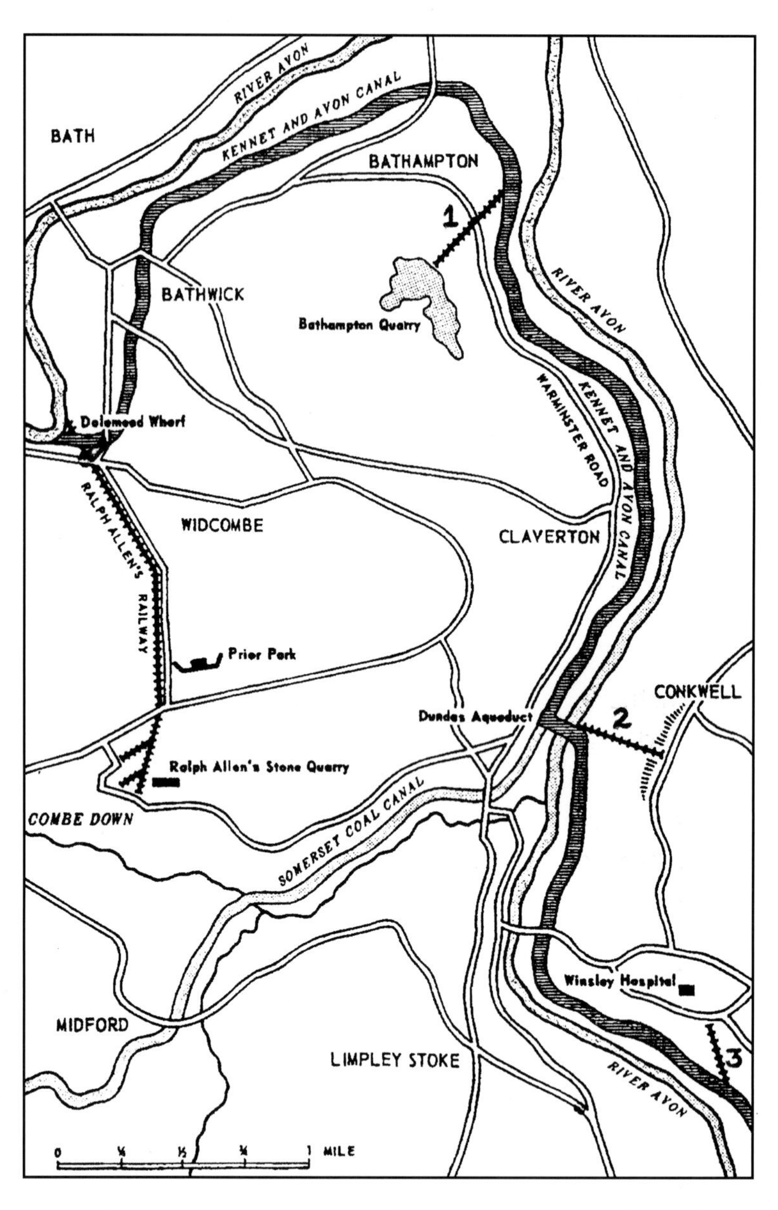

1. Bathampton Incline to the canal at Holcombe Farm.
2. Conkwell Incline to the east end of Dundas Aqueduct.
3. Murhill Incline from Winsley to the canal between Dundas and Avoncliff.

It is not known whether stone from Ralph Allen's quarry was used for the construction of the Widcombe flight of locks or indeed for any other works built of stone in the Bath area, but it is certain that if it was, it would have had to have been transported by road. His pioneering railway, the first ever to use cast-iron, flanged wheels, which ran from his quarries on Combe Down to Allen's Wharf at Dolemead, very close to the junction of the canal with the River Avon, had been dismantled in about 1765, though stone may still have been brought down by road for use on the canal.

Mason's Marks

In 1918 Major Gorham of the Somerset Masters Lodge made a study of the various Banker marks, commonly called Masons' marks, found scattered over the Avoncliff and Dundas aqueducts and the Sydney Gardens tunnels, but less frequently on other stone structures on the canal. His paper, *The K.ennet and Avon Canal and its Marks,* makes interesting reading. These marks are to be found on the faces of the voussoirs, on both sides of the parapet and on numerous stones of the arch faces and abutment walls, on ashlar and rusticated courses alike.

> Most of the marks are undoubtedly those of the Operative stone Masons who cut the stone and such marks are preferably called "Banker Marks." There are, however, many other examples of small marks which are assuredly marks of approval or "passing" the work, and the Greek cross is undoubtedly used for this purpose in the canal works, as are also the triangle and square. The large mark, to be found on the North-west parapet capstones, is of a different order, and is probably a Guild or Lodge mark, though

it is true that such a mark was used by the old Operatives as a "foundation mark" denoting the proportion of the building. The mark ⊥ was quite possibly an approval mark, and in the case of the second bridge at Bradford we must either assume that it was so used or that one mason made very nearly the whole of the voussoirs of the bridge by himself; this would have taken one man so long to do that it is improbable.

It is perhaps interesting to note that the majority of the marks conform to the proportion of a 3,4,5 triangle. A set-square was part of every mason's set of tools and it would be a simple matter for a mason to carve his personal mark on a completed block using a square of these proportions. Even the five-pointed star can be drawn by this method, with only a small amount of error. There were various kinds of marks used by the old Operative Masons. A stone coming from the quarry would have a number and bed mark, but these would be erased during dressing at the mason's yard or on site. Major Gorham further states that:

Marks were further broadly divided into two classes, viz., Square Masons' marks and Arch Masons' marks, and, generally speaking, whenever a mark is curved or has curves in it, that mark is an Arch Mason's mark, or has come down from Arch Masons in the past.

Then we have the operative mark of the man who cuts the stone: this is the "banker mark." It is stated that banker marks are still in use, and so they are; but the statement requires considerable qualification. The present state of affairs is this, that some masons have banker marks and some have not and the reason is that the system of requiring masons to *have* banker marks and *use* them died out just ten years ago.

Next we have masters and overseers' approval marks (but "overseers" were super fellows and super fellow erectors).

There were also Division Marks; Basis Marks; Wall Marks (*i.e.* N, S, E and W); Period Marks; Construction Marks (e.g., position marks); Course Marks; Inside and Outside Marks; Proportion Marks; the latter was usually the foundation or "Jesod" Mark.

Construction and Course Marks are the only marks other than Banker Marks which survive today in common use, and these will both be found on the top bed of the stone.

Among the stones of the Avoncliff Aqueduct are many with two marks, but one of them will generally be found to be the square, the triangle or the Greek cross, and in two instances there are three marks on the one face [see above, opposite].

This is not very extraordinary, but when we come to more than one complicated mark on one face it would look as if two masons were employed cutting one stone.

On the centre of the parapet coping in the Avoncliff Aqueduct are placed two large blocks for architectural appearance, one on either side. They measure 7ft. 8in. long by 1ft. 1½in. broad by 10in. deep and are both similarly marked with two marks. There are also two such stones on the Dundas Aqueduct [see the photograph on the previous page].

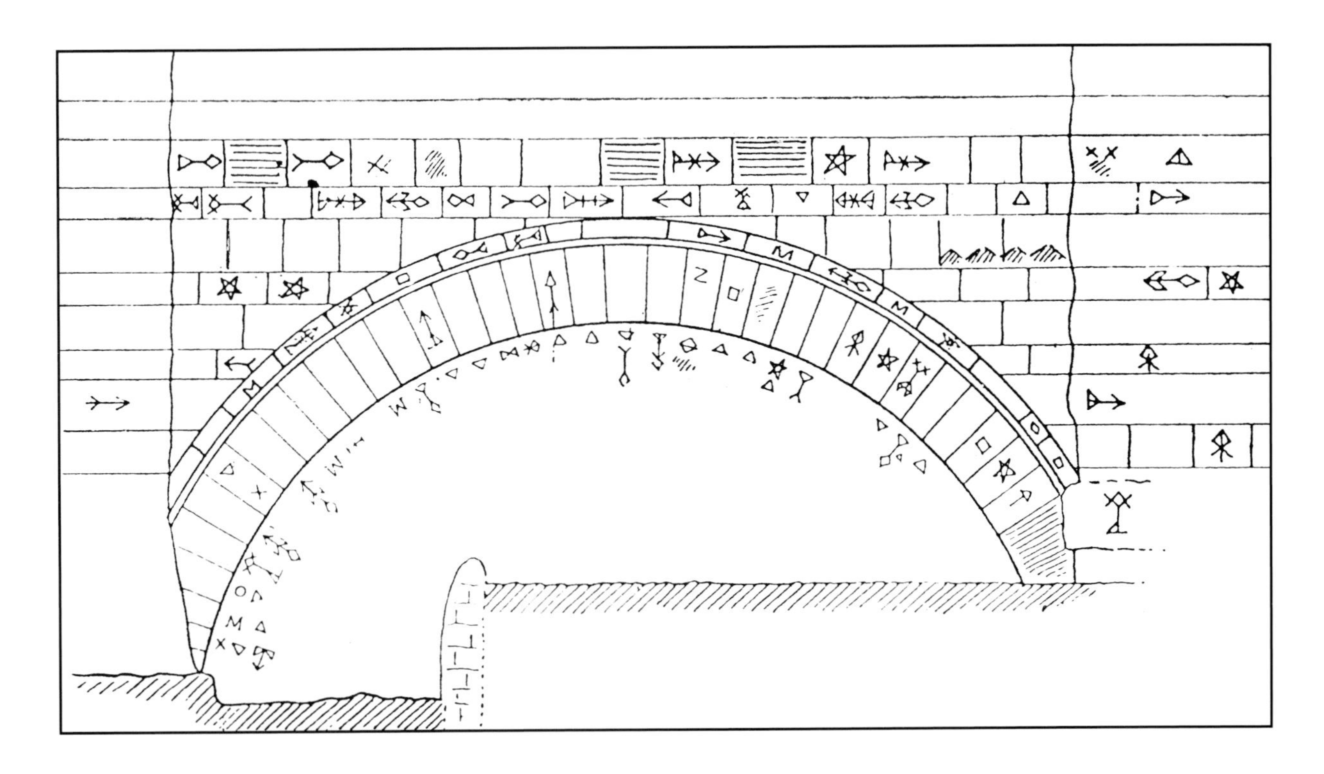

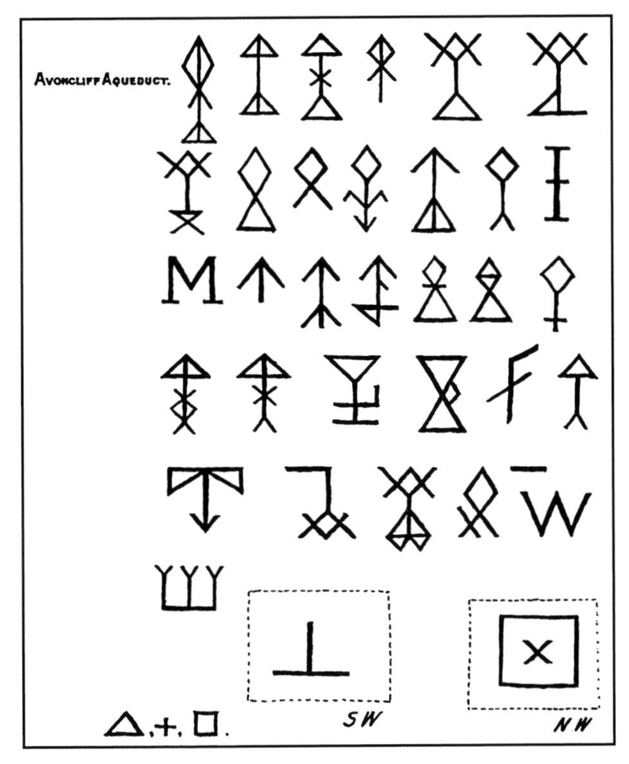
AVONCLIFF AQUEDUCT.
SW
NW

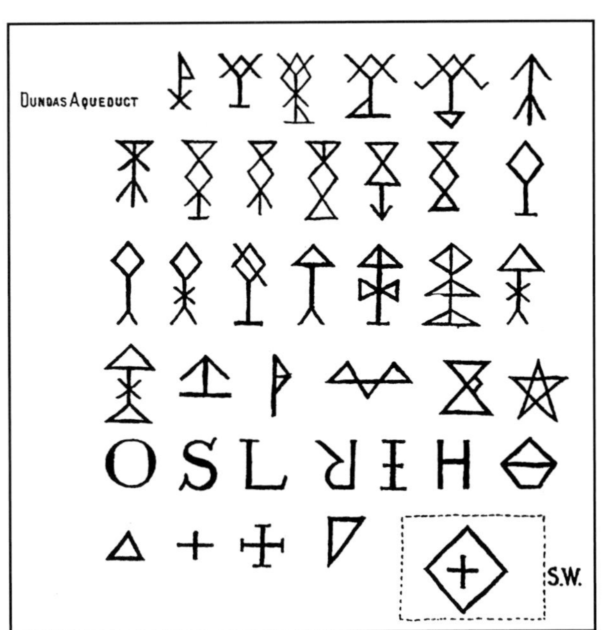
DUNDAS AQUEDUCT
S.W.

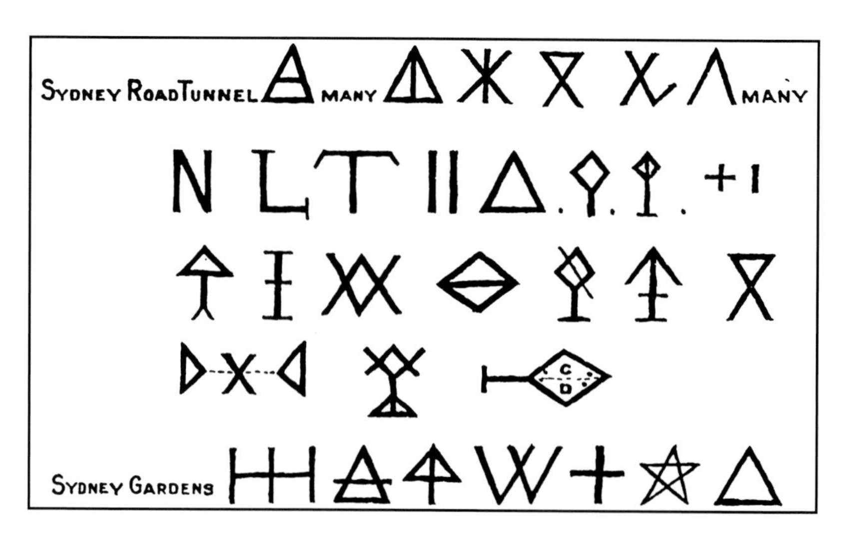

Major Gorham also tried to find out the identity of the masons employed during the construction of the canal. Records of the contracts for constructional work were thought to be contained in the papers of the Company, originally kept at *Cleveland House*. These papers were transferred to the GWR's offices in Paddington when the railway company took over the canal, but were subsequently 'lost'. It is now, therefore, practically impossible to discover who the masons were who worked on the canal. Major Gorham traced one particular mark to a Bristol family and noticed that others were similar to those recorded. He also states that there was a tradition among operatives in his day (1918) that Scottish masons were called in during the construction of the stonework on the canal, particularly the large aqueducts. He also mentions that there were Operative Stone Masons working in the stoneyards near Bath who had banker marks similar to those in question. It is conceivable that he was able to talk with some of the older men who remembered their fathers talking about the construction of the canal; but this clue is not much help and only a considerable amount of research into the archives of the various masonic lodges will yield any solution to the puzzle.

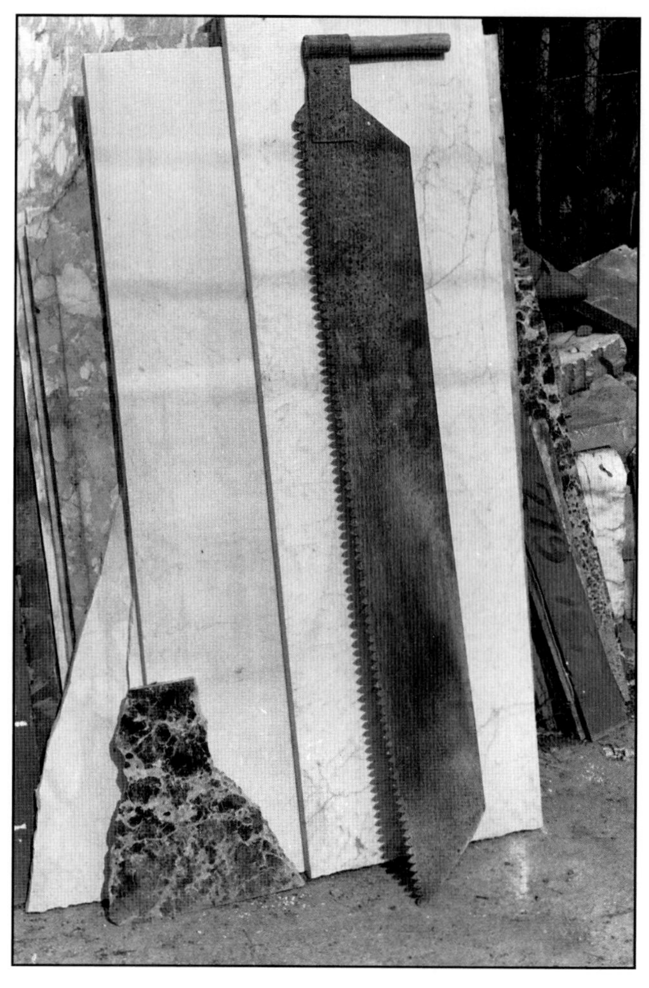

Canalia

There are many fittings, which are an integral part of the canal scene, and are therefore worth a mention. Anyone walking along the tow-path may be puzzled by short lengths of railway line protruding from the ground at intervals. Occasionally these posts have a piece of board roughly nine inches square attached, with a number on them, either painted, or in metal. These indicated the GWR gang number assigned to that section of the canal for maintenance work. Likewise,

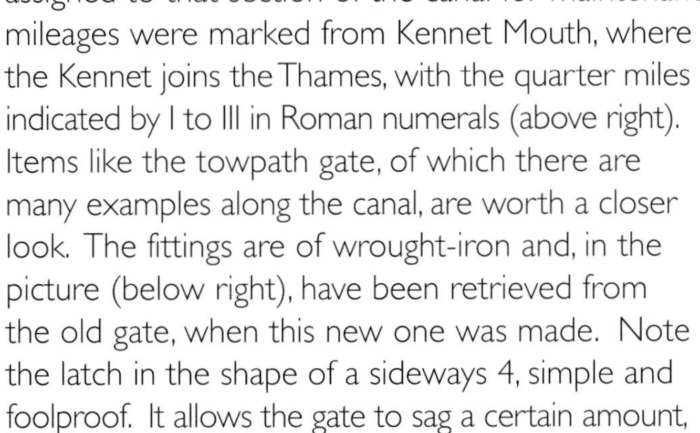

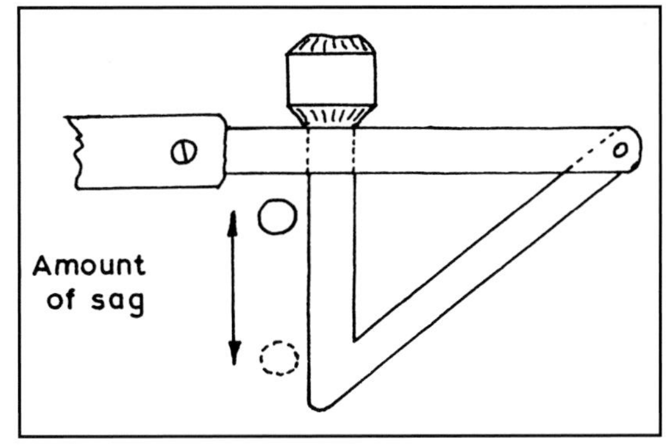

mileages were marked from Kennet Mouth, where the Kennet joins the Thames, with the quarter miles indicated by I to III in Roman numerals (above right). Items like the towpath gate, of which there are many examples along the canal, are worth a closer look. The fittings are of wrought-iron and, in the picture (below right), have been retrieved from the old gate, when this new one was made. Note the latch in the shape of a sideways 4, simple and foolproof. It allows the gate to sag a certain amount, but after that it will be resting on the ground and will have to be rehung. The top strap goes through the upright and is bolted to the top rail in several places, thus spreading the load. The bottom strap is U-shaped, which reduces any tendency for the gate heel to kick sideways when weight is put on the other end of the gate, as when a person climbs over it. The far end is protected at the top by an iron band as shown.

The fittings of the locks are also of interest. Shown below is a lock gate retaining strap, which holds the gate upright, while allowing it to pivot freely. As mentioned earlier, the cast-iron frame is held in place by staples and molten lead. There are at least two different designs of frame in use on this canal, but both perform the same function. The stone block into which it was set was usually stapled to its neighbours by tie-bars for extra strength. When the gate was lowered into position a collar was loosely attached to the framework with metal wedges, allowing the gate to pivot freely. At the heel of the gate was a hemispherical iron button, which turned in a cup of larger diameter than the button, to allow for plenty of play. Water pressure would then move the gate to produce a watertight fit between the heel post and the hollow quoin in the lock wall. Above, a lock gate can be seen in course of construction in the Devizes workshops; the size and type of joints can be seen clearly. The tenon for the balance beam, since removed, is shown in the photograph on the right.

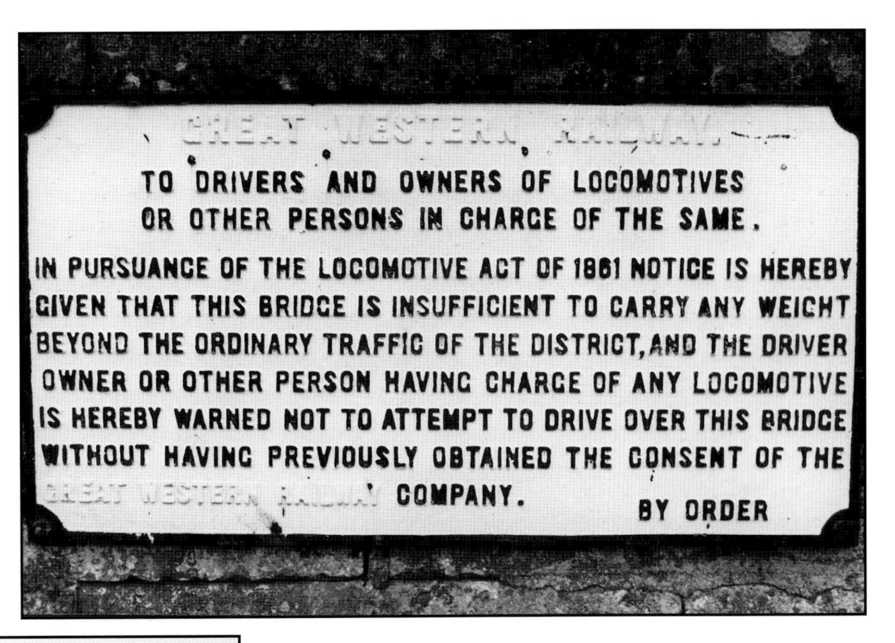

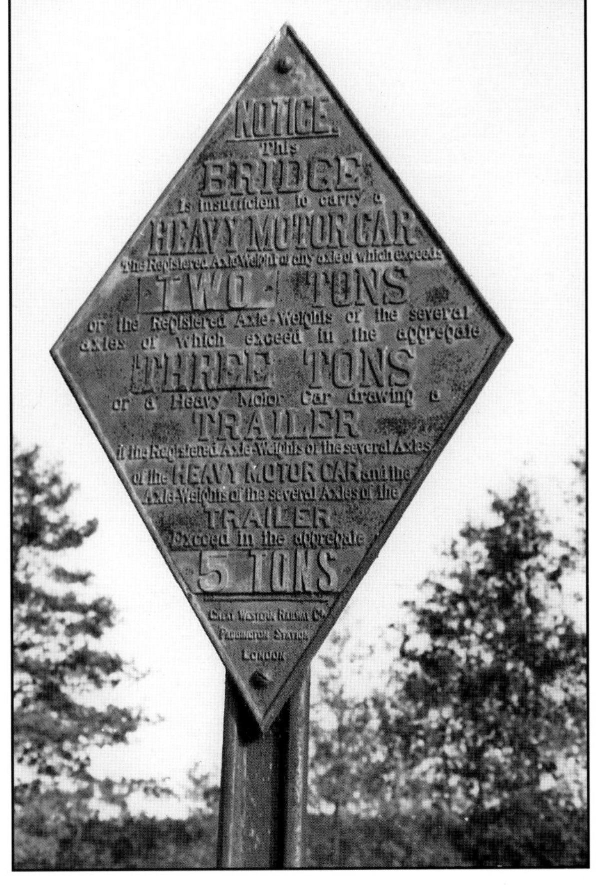

These photographs show two examples of notices erected by the GWR, both of which occur frequently along the canal. The cast-iron diamond-shaped plate is a familiar sight at the approaches to practically every bridge on the canal. In this example, a warning is given that the bridge will not support more than a certain weight, so that the driver of any heavy vehicle is left in no doubt as to whether it is safe to use the bridge or not. As a point of interest, an overbridge on the Birmingham Canal Navigations, limited to 5 tons weight, was tested to destruction and finally collapsed under a load of 110 tons. The wording of the notice above is looser and more threatening. "The ordinary traffic of the district" might be interpreted as meaning 20-ton lorries from nearby flour mills, and "without having previously obtained the consent of the company" implies a lengthy correspondence.

Because the paddles on the K&A were stiff, long-throw windlasses, or lock keys, were developed for working the locks. The three types used are shown above, being a left-hand and a right-hand key and a small one which was used to speed up the winding down of each paddle.

The limit of land owned by the canal company was marked by boundary stones, in which was incised the letters KA (right). Examples of these boundary markers can be seen at Claverton Pumping Station and at Crofton, in the leat leading from the pump outlets. The GWR, as was to be expected, used cast-iron boundary markers in the form of discs on top of short posts, rather like large drawing pins.

Condition of the Structures in 1964

Mileages are taken from Nicholas Hammond's *Kennet and Avon Waterway: The Complete Chart.* They are in miles and tenths of a mile, measuring from the canal's junction with the River Thames.

Mileage	Item	Comments
19.4	Newbury Bridge	Stone, good condition
19.5	Newbury Lock, No.85	Excellent condition, all gates and paddles o.k.
19.6	West Mills Swing Bridge	Roving, wood, standard K&A design, good condition
19.8	Northcroft Footbridge	Cast-iron with concrete bases; guide rails for boats provided; water main also goes over
20.2	Railway Bridge (Lambourn Valley branch line)	Brick support to girder
20.4	Enborne Bridge	Roving, brick, stone capped, good condition
20.4	Guyer's Lock, No.84	Good condition, wooden gates with steel beams
20.8	Overfall Weir	Brick, patched with cement, wooden plank walkway
20.9	Higg's Lock, No.83	Good condition, wooden gates & beams
21.2	Pickletimber Railway Bridge (main line, W.R.)	Brick on east side; girder main span; stone with arches on west side for stream & flood waters; skew arch of brick with stone facing only
21.5	Benham Bridge	Brick, stone capped, good condition
21.5	Benham Lock, No.82	Good condition, wooden gates; lower pair steel beams; one top ground paddle only
21.8	Overfall Weir	Recently repaired new concrete towpath, bridge & railings; brick arches remaining
21.9	River Kennet Weir	Brick culverts, overlaid with railway lines to carry towpath; wooden handrails
22.4	Hamstead Wharf	Little depth of water
22.5	Hamstead Bridge	Brick, cement capped, good condition
22.6	Hamstead Lock, No.81	Silted up; wooden gates, no beams on top pair
22.6	Overflow Weir	Wooden sluice gear, new & in good condition
22.9	Copse Lock, No.80	All gates rotted; one lower gate beam o.k.
23.3	Dreweat's Lock Bridge	Brick, stone capped, good condition
23.3	Dreweat's Lock, No.79	All paddle gear o.k.; lower gates derelict; top gates o.k.
23.3	Overfall Weirs	Circular, brick
24.2	Shepherd's Bridge	Brick, good condition

24.8	*Dundas Arms* & Wharf	In use as hotel; present garages once stables
24.8	Lengthman's Cottage	Inhabited
24.8	Kintbury Bridge	Brick abutments; girder arch; iron railings
24.9	Kintbury Lock, No.78	No bottom gates; top gates beams missing
25.2	Vicarage Bridge	Brick, supported by rails on west side; stone towline protection deeply grooved
25.4	Orchard Meadow Bridge	Brick; stone towline protection; patched underside of arch
25.8	Brunsden's Lock Bridge	Brick, patched with cement
25.8	Brunsden's Lock, No.77	Beams broken on lower gates; top gates beams missing; lock wall patched with cement
26.2	Railway Bridge	Fairly new girder & brick; original stone abutments remaining & circular iron girders left standing in canal
26.4	Wire Lock Bridge	Brick, good condition
26.4	Wire Lock, No.76	Brick, cement capped lock wall, top gates badly patched; one top gate beam missing; all paddle gear o.k.
27.2	Dunmill Lock Bridge	Roving, brick, stone capped
27.2	Dunmill Lock, No.75	Paddle gear o.k.; lower gates o.k.; top gates rotted with brick dam behind; pillbox on south side approach
27.3	Old Mill	Inhabited, in good condition
27.8	Station Road Footbridge	Brick piers, girder & timber replacement of swing bridge, new, full navigational height
28.0	Hungerford Bridge	Red & grey brick, stone-capped, good condition
28.0	Hungerford Wharf	Iron footbridges over towpath approaches on south side
28.2	Hungerford Lock, No.74	Walls stone capped; top gates o.k.; bottom gates rotted; one beam o.k. on towpath side
28.4	Hungerford Church Swing Bridge	Wooden, standard K&A pattern
29.0	Hungerford Marsh Lock, No.73	Brick, stone capping; bottom gates o.k.; beams missing on top gates; paddles o.k.; swing bridge across lock in good condition
29.3	Cobblers Lock, No.72	Lock & cottage in good condition; beams and handrails painted; small footbridge at tail of lock
29.3	Dun Aqueduct	Brick, three oval low arches
29.5	Barrackfield Swing Bridge	Wood, unpainted, fair condition
29.6	Railway Bridge	Brick abutments, stone protected; girder arch
29.7	Picketfield Lock, No.71	Brick, stone capped; bottom gates rotted, beams o.k.; top gates o.k., one beam only

30.2	Picketfield Swing Bridge	Replaced by unsafe wooden footbridge to nearby pig farm
30.3	Froxfield Bridge	Brick, standard pattern; stone protection at arch base
30.4	Froxfield Lower Lock, No.70	Brick, stone capped; bottom gates beyond repair; brick dam behind top gates
30.6	Froxfield Upper Lock, No.69	Brick, stone capped; bottom gates beyond repair; top gates & one beam o.k.; ground paddles o.k.
30.8	Siphon Culvert	Brick, over River Dun
30.8	Oakhill Down Bridge	Brick, standard pattern; tank blocks nearby
30.8	Oakhill Down Lock, No.68	Brick, stone capped; bottom gates beyond repair; beams missing on top gates
31.3	Fore Bridge	Brick; three T-shaped ties in arch top; patched with blue brick; cottage nearby
31.7	Little Bedwyn Footbridge	Iron; crosses railway & canal
31.7	Little Bedwyn Lock, No.67	Brick, stone capped; all gates & beams beyond repair; brick dam top end; pound below badly silted
31.8	Little Bedwyn Bridge	Brick piers & abutments; girder spans across railway & canal
32.1	Potter's Lock, No.66	Brick, stone capped; bottom gates o.k.; top gates present but one beam only with handrail; old sluice gear on far bank
32.5	Burnt Mill Lock, No.65	Brick, stone capped; gates o.k.; top gates with one beam only; standard swing bridge across lock middle in need of repair
32.8	Bedwyn Wharf Bridge	Brick, standard pattern; patched underside of arch
33.2	Bedwyn Church Bridge	Brick over lock tail; stream enters canal below lock, forming silt delta
33.2	Bedwyn Church Lock, No.64	Brick, stone capped; bottom gates o.k.; brick dam at top end; gates beyond repair
33.4	Mill Bridge	Brick, standard pattern; flood weir on towpath side just below bridge
33.4	Stonemason's Cottage	Flint walls, stone corners
33.8	Beech Tree Walk Bridge	Brick, good condition
33.8	Crofton Bottom Lock, No.63	Brick, stone capped; bottom gates beyond repair; top gates brand new, but with no beams; ground paddles new & locked
34.0	Column Ride Bridge	Brick, stone capped; skew arch balustrade missing in places; tree growing in middle of track & tank blocks

34.1	Crofton Lock, No.62	Brick, stone capped; bottom gates poor, but beams & paddle gear present; top gates o.k. & beams in place
34.5	Crofton Bridge	Brick, stone capped
34.5	Crofton Lock, No.61	Brick, stone capped; bottom gates beyond repair; top gates patched & beams propped up
34.7	Outlet from Wilton Water	Wooden sluice gear set in stone & brick framework
34.7	Crofton Pumping Station	Stone; slate tiled roof; brick chimney on east side
34.7	Crofton Lock, No.60	Brick, stone capped; gates in poor condition; paddle gear o.k.; pound above almost dry
34.8	Crofton Lock, No.59	Brick, stone capped; all gates in poor condition but paddle gear present; chamber dry
35.0	Freewarren Bridge	Brick, standard pattern, good condition
35.0	Crofton Lock, No.58	Brick, cement capped walls; top gates poor, all gear & beams present; pound above full of water
35.2	Crofton Lock, No.57	Brick, cement capped walls; paddle gear present; all beams broken
35.4	Crofton Lock, No.56	Brick, cement capped walls; paddle gear o.k.; all beams broken; bottom gates useless
35.5	Wolfhall Fields Bridge	Brick, cement capped, repaired recently
35.5	Crofton Top Lock, No.55	Brick, all gates beyond repair; paddle gear present; stop planks in place to hold water in summit pound
35.6	Railway Bridge (Midland & S.W. Junction Railway)	Brick abutments only remaining
35.8	Wolfhall Bridge	Brick, standard pattern cement capped; no protection at towpath level
36.4	Bruce Tunnel, East End	Brick, stone capped; large stone plaque above portal; no stone protection at boat & towpath level
36.7	Bruce Tunnel, West End	Brick, stone capped; large stone plaque above portal (uninscribed); no protection at boat & towpath level; south approach wall being rebuilt (October 1964)
37.3	Burbage Wharf Bridge	Brick, stone capped, standard pattern; enlarged to cross deep cutting; slight skew arch
37.3	Burbage Wharf	Former warehouse, inhabited; old wooden crane in place
38.1	Wootton Rivers Top Lock, No.54	Brick, stone capped; gates in fair condition; top beams broken, bottom beams o.k.; all paddle gear present; inhabited cottage on offside

38.1	Cadley Bridge	Brick, stone capped
38.3	Wootton Rivers Lock, No.53	Brick, stone capped; top gates holding water but beams collapsed; bottom gates o.k.; all paddle gear present
38.3	Brimslade Bridge	Brick, stone capped
38.7	Wootton Rivers Lock, No.52	Brick, stone capped; top gates o.k. though beams much patched; all paddle gear in place; one bottom gate o.k
38.7	Heathy Close Bridge	Brick, stone capped, good condition; no towpath
38.9	Overflow Weir	Stream enters on towpath side & overflows into original bed on north side through three square stone culverts
39.0	Wootton Rivers Bottom Lock, No.51	Brick, stone capped; all beams collapsed; top gates o.k.; bottom gates collapsed; paddle gear ok; lock cottage on south side inhabited
39.0	Wootton Rivers Bridge	Unusually high to road on same level; brick, stone capped; overflow discharges below bridge on north side; towing grooves on bridge coping; no towpath under bridge
39.2	Wootton Rivers Farm Bridge	Brick, stone capped
39.4	Carrel Crown Bridge	Brick, stone capped; anti-tank blocks on top
40.0	New Mill Bridge	Brick, stone capped, well patched with brick and pointed; stop planks
40.0	New Mill Wharf	Small lay-by on towpath side; no buildings
40.2	Culvert	Brick, under embankment
40.7	Milkhouse Water Bridge	Brick, stone capped; stop gates on both sides of bridge those on towpath side missing, other two rotten
41.1	Culvert	Brick, under embankment
41.4	Pain's Bridge	Brick, stone capped; double stop gates rotten; anti-tank blocks on towpath on both sides
41.8	Pewsey Wharf	Brick walls, stone capped; brick warehouse, south end inhabited; rest of wharf open & unused
41.8	Pewsey Bridge	Brick skew arch, stone capped; double stop gates, towpath side missing, others rotted
42.4	Bristow Bridge	Roving, blue brick, stone capped; parapet has four recessed panels; stop planks provided nearby
42.8	Stowell Park Suspension Bridge	Iron suspension bridge, with "Dredge Patentee Bath" cast in both chain support towers
43.1	Wilcot Bridge	Brick faced, grey rubble stone underside of arch

43.3	Wilcot Swing Bridge	Wooden, standard pattern
43.5	Bowden's Bridge	Brick, stone capped
43.9	Lady's Bridge	Stone, decorated facing on brick base; part of balustrade coping on east side missing; two pillars missing from balustrade on south-west side; protective roller missing; stop planks in rack nearby.
44.5	Lambit Swing Bridge	Missing; remains of iron work of bearings present
44.9	Woodborough Fields Bridge	Roving, brick, stone capped, iron rod bridge; arch protection on east side only
45.3	Ford Swing Bridge	Missing; ironwork remains in heap on offside
45.6	Alton Valley Bridge	Brick, stone capped
45.7	Sluice	Wooden, set in brick; feeder & flood relief to & from stream
45.7	Culvert	Brick, under embankment
45.7	Windlass	Wooden roller supported by railway line posts
45.8	Honeystreet Bridge	Brick, stone capped
45.9	Honeystreet Wharf	Brick walls, stone capped; wooden crane post; wooden tower with clock on top (not working); houses inhabited; wooden barge-building sheds adjacent, derelict
46.0	*Barge Inn*	Substantial building with several outhouses of brick & wood
46.5	Stanton Bridge	Brick, stone capped
46.8	England's Bridge	Brick, stone capped; stop grooves & planks present
47.7	All Cannings Bridge	Brick, stone capped; stop grooves & planks present
47.9	Woodway Bridge	Brick, stone capped; stop grooves & planks present
48.6	Allington Swing Bridge	Wooden footbridge, newly repaired & painted
48.8	Allington Bridge	Brick, stone capped; stop grooves & planks present
49.3	Horton Fields Swing Bridge	Wooden, standard pattern, newly painted
50.0	Horton Chain Bridge	Brick, stone capped; parapet built up on east side to follow line of road
50.6	Culvert	Sump for stream with overflow weir into meadow
50.7	Bishop's Cannings Swing Bridge	Wood, standard pattern, newly installed & painted
51.2	Horton Bridge	Brick, stone capped; *Bridge Inn* nearby
51.8	Lay Wood Bridge	Brick, stone capped; blue brick base of arch
52.7	Coates Bridge	Brick, across cutting so line of parapet horizontal
53.0	Brickham Bridge	Brick, across cutting so line of parapet horizontal; blue brick balustrade on north side

53.4	London Road Bridge	Stone, patched with brick
53.7	Park Road Bridge	Stone, patched with brick
53.8	Cemetery Road Bridge	Roving, stone, patched with brick; former towpath entrance to wharf blocked off
53.8	Devizes Wharf	Stables converted to garages, rest of wharf area a car park
53.9	Devizes Top Lock, No.50	Stop planks in place; new top gates without beams; brick stone capped walls; one beam broken on bottom gates
54.1	Devizes Town Bridge	Roving, fine stone bridge; towpath tunnel at lock tail
54.2	Devizes Lock, No.49	Brick, stone capped; top gates new, no beams; bottom gates beyond repair; one badly fire damaged
54.3	Devizes Lock, No.48	Top gates o.k. but beam broken on towpath side; bottom gate on towpath side collapsed
54.4	Devizes Lock, No.47	Top gates o.k. but beam broken on towpath side; bottom gate on towpath side beyond repair
54.4	Prison Bridge	Brick, parapet replaced by railings over arch & towpath tunnel; cast-iron protection at entrances to stone-lined tunnel; plaque on west side
54.4	Devizes Lock, No.46	Top gates rotted, beams broken; bottom gates o.k.
54.5	Devizes Lock, No.45	Top gates rotted, beam on towpath side patched other broken; bottom gates nearside beyond repair, offside beam broken
54.6	Caen Hill Lock, No.44	Water level in pound above 3 feet below normal; top gates badly patched, beams o.k.; bottom gates missing
54.7	Devizes Yard Bridge	Girder with steel railings; over lock tail to cottage
54.7	Caen Hill Lock, No.43	Top gates o.k., offside beam snapped; bottom gates o.k.; watchman's bothy at lock tail
54.8	Caen Hill Lock, No.42	All pounds dry below lock 43; top gates rotted, nearside beam o.k.; bottom gates o.k. but beam broken on towpath side
54.8	Caen Hill Lock, No.41	Top gates & beams beyond repair; bottom gates o.k.
54.9	Caen Hill Lock, No.40	Top gates o.k., beams rotted; bottom gates & beams beyond repair
55.0	Caen Hill Lock, No.39	Top gates beyond repair; bottom gates o.k., but beam broken on towpath side

55.0	Caen Hill Lock, No.38	Top gates beyond repair, beams possibly o.k.; bottom gates o.k., but beams missing
55.1	Caen Hill Lock, No.37	Top gates beyond repair; bottom gates o.k., but near beam broken and far beam missing
55.2	Caen Hill Lock, No.36	Top gates beyond repair; bottom gate nearside o.k., offside beyond repair, both beams broken
55.2	Caen Hill Lock, No.35	Top gates beyond repair; bottom gates o.k., but both beams broken
55.3	Caen Hill Lock, No.34	Top gates beyond repair; bottom gates o.k., but offside beam broken
55.3	Caen Hill Lock, No.33	Top gates o.k., but offside beam broken; bottom gates o.k.
55.4	Caen Hill Lock, No.32	Top gates beyond repair; bottom gate nearside badly burnt, beam broken on other gate
55.4	Caen Hill Lock, No.31	Top offside gate o.k., other beyond repair, both beams broken; bottom gates & beams o.k.
55.5	Caen Hill Lock, No.30	Top gates beyond repair, beams o.k., sill rotted; bottom gates o.k.
55.5	Caen Hill Lock, No.29	Top gates sagging, offside beam sawn off short; bottom gates o.k., both beams broken; watchman's bothy on far bank; water in pound below
55.6	Caen Hill Lock, No.28	Top gates o.k.; bottom towpath side gate beyond repair, other o.k., both beams collapsed
55.6	Upper Foxhangers Bridge	Brick, stone capped; towpath tunnel stone-lined,; bridge on towpath side of stone up to level of tunnel arch base; nearby house of same vintage; bridge protected by stone at water level
55.7	Devizes Lock, No.27	Top gates new but no beams; bottom gates missing; water up to normal level
55.7	Devizes Lock, No.26	Top gates & beams o.k.; beam rotted on bottom gate on towpath side
55.8	Devizes Lock, No.25	Top gates new but no beams; bottom gates beyond repair; water level 3 feet below normal above & below lock
55.9	Devizes Lock, No.24	Top gates o.k., but beams collapsed; bottom gates o.k.
56.1	Devizes Lock, No.23	All gates rotted, all beams collapsed except top on towpath side; water 4 feet below normal

56.1	Foxhangers Footbridge	Brick piers & timber arch, replacing former swing bridge; pound 1 foot below normal
56.2	Devizes Lock, No.22	Top gates rotted; bottom gates & beams all o.k.
56.2	Lower Foxhangers Bridge	Roving, brick; former tramroad tunnel on south side; concrete anti-tank blocks; parapets replaced by iron railings; arch repaired
56.2	Railway Bridge	Stone abutments to girder arch supported by 3 piers of concrete blocks
56.4	Summerham Aqueduct	Stone portals to culvert for Summerham Brook
56.5	Summerham Brook Feeder	Enters on north (towpath) side under level bridge supported by railway lines
56.8	Martinslade Bridge	Roving, blue brick on east side; north end parapet built up to road level; underside of arch with stone patching; west side stone with extensive red brick patching; stone parapet; iron towline protection present
57.2	Sell's Green Bridge	Stone, extensively patched with red brick
57.5	Sell's Green Valley Swing Bridge	Wood with iron rails & splash boards
57.7	Rusty Lane Swing Bridge	Wood, standard pattern
58.0	Seend Top Lock, No.21	Top gates sagging; bottom gates o.k.; stop planks in rack; lock cottage of stone with tiled roof
58.0	Seend Selver Bridge	Stone, much patched with red brick on west side
58.2	Seend Lock, No.20	Top gates o.k. but beams gone; bottom gates o.k., beams gone; far lock wall badly cracked at meeting of patching with original wall
58.3	Seend Lock, No.19	Top gates sagging, towpath-side beam broken; bottom gates o.k.
58.3	Seend Wharf Bridge	Blue brick, except over arch, where parapet replaced by corrugated iron with brick supporting piers; stone towline protection; abutments of former tramroad bridge to Seend Ironworks & quarries
58.4	Seend Wharf	Two large houses in private use, one a pub; stone with slate roofs
58.5	Seend Lock, No.18	Top gates sagging, far beam sawn off; bottom gates o.k. but towpath-side beam sawn off
58.5	Seend Lock Bridge	Stone, patched with blue brick completely on east side; much patched with red & blue brick on west side

58.7	Seend Bottom Lock, No.17	Top gates o.k. but both beams sawn off; bottom gates beyond repair, beams o.k.; chains for opening gates
59.2	Seend Park Swing Bridge	Wooden footbridge, standard pattern; newly painted railing
59.6	Lowes Swing Bridge	Wooden footbridge, standard pattern
59.7	Melksham Park Swing Bridge	Wooden, iron railings
60.1	Newtown Swing Bridge	Wooden, iron railings; splash boards
60.3	Barrett's Lock, No.16	Top gates o.k.; bottom gates o.k., towpath-side beam missing, offside beam sawn off; stop planks nearby
60.5	Buckley's Lock, No.15	Top gates patched; towpath-side beam supported; handrails on all gates; bottom gates & beams o.k.; bridge to lock cottage across lock tail; stop grooves in lock tail
60.6	Junction House	Stone, inhabited; toll office extension on east end
60.6	Semington Bridge	Stone, heavily patched with red & blue brick on both faces & arch; stone parapet o.k.
60.6	Semington Wharf	Stone walls to wharf; stone house inhabited; wharf area now a garden
60.7	Semington Aqueduct	Stone, patched with blue brick; large uninscribed stone plaques on both sides, anti-tank blocks on towpath
61.0	Semington Swing Bridge	Wooden, standard pattern; stop gates o.k.
61.7	Whaddon Grove Bridge	Red & blue brick, stone-capped; protected at towpath level
61.8	Whaddon Bridge	Rebuilt; stone abutments; girder arch; blue brick parapet
62.4	Hilperton Marsh Swing Bridge No.2	Wooden, standard pattern.
62.6	Hilperton Marsh Swing Bridge No.1	Wooden, standard pattern
62.9	Marsh Wharf	Stone walls; stables & all buildings inhabited
63.0	Hilperton Bridge	Stone, patched with brick on underside of arch
63.1	Hilperton Wharf	Cottage, inhabited
63.4	Parson's Bridge	Stone, arch mostly brick-patched, stop gates on east side o.k.
63.5	Culvert	Stone; portal surmounted by stone wall on west side
63.6	Ball's Bridge	Stone, patched with blue and red brick, 3 stop planks only
63.6	Ladydown Aqueduct	Stone, over railway

63.7	Biss Aqueduct	Stone, patched with yellow brick; wide enough for towpath on both sides of canal
63.9	Ladydown Bridge	Stone, much patched with red brick; stop gates on west side o.k.; east side ones rotted
65.0	Widbrook Bridge	Stone, patched with red brick; both pairs of stop gates beyond repair
65.7	Bradford Wharf	Stone walls, stone building with boat cover & dry dock
65.7	Bradford Deep Lock, No.14	All gates o.k.; red brick walls, 3 courses of stone at top; toll office stone with slate roof
65.7	Bradford Lock Bridge	Stone; no towpath provision
66.4	Bradford Swing Bridge	New swing bridge to sewage works, no trusses; double stop gates, both rotted
67.3	Stop Gates	Good condition, holding back water up to Bradford Deep Lock
67.4	Stone Windlass for drainage plug & stone towing post	
67.4	Avoncliff buildings	Stone, slate roofs
67.4	Avoncliff Aqueduct	Roving, stone, 3 arches; central arch sagged; de-watered
67.4	Railway Aqueduct	Stone
67.5	Stop Gates	Both gates missing; two stop planks only
67.7	Winsley Bridge	Stone, slightly patched blue & red brick; plug windlass nearby, both pairs stop gates beyond repair
68.1	Lengthman's Cottage	Stone, tiled roof; inhabited; both pairs of stop gates missing
68.5	Stop Gates	All stop planks present
68.6	Stop Gates	Stop gates missing; no stop planks
69.1	Limpley Stoke Bridge	Stone, repaired with stone; stop gates present; south pair beyond repair, north pair new & holding back water
69.5	Stop Gates	Fair condition; lengthman's cottage stone with slate roof, dated 1895
69.9	Dundas Aqueduct	Stone, 3 arches; south face in good condition; north face much patched with blue brick; east arch showing evidence of leaking
70.0	Dundas Wharf	Stone walls; iron crane; barge alongside (sunk); toll house & square store, stone with slate roofs
70.0	Dundas Bridge	Roving, stone abutments; iron girder arch; wooden lattice railings; stop planks in place; stop gates rotted

70.5	Millbrook Swing Bridge	Wooden, standard pattern; stop grooves; planks in place
70.6	Sheepwash Feeder	Stone overflow weir; stream enters canal nearby
71.0	Stop Grooves	Stop planks in use acting as temporary footbridge to farm
71.2	Claverton Bridge	Stone, good condition
71.3	Claverton Pumping Station	Stone walls, slate roofs
71.3	Claverton Sluice Gear	Wooden; stone bridge over a feeder from the Avon
71.3	Pump Attendant's House	Stone, tiled roof
71.5	Harding's Bridge	Stone, good condition; stop planks present; iron towline protection on north side only
72.2	Stop Grooves	Stop planks in place
72.5	Holcombe Swing Bridge, Hampton Quarry Wharf	Wooden, standard pattern; double stop gates o.k.; nearby lengthman's cottage inhabited, stone with slate roof
73.1	Bathampton Bridge	Stone, good condition; iron towline protection on both sides
73.1	Canal Cottages	Stone, fronting onto towpath
73.4	Stop Groove	Two stop planks remaining
73.6	Candy's Bridge	Stone, good condition; both parapets continue the line of the road on south-east side
74.0	Folly's Foot Swing Bridge	Footbridge, standard pattern, good condition stop gates on west side o.k., those on east side beyond repair
74.4	Darlington Wharf	Stone house, originally start of 'Scotch' boat to Bradford
74.4	Sydney Gardens No.2 Tunnel	Stone, good condition; north portal plain; south portal highly decorated; tunnel has masons' marks & towpath; stone throughout with some brick patching at water level
74.5	Footbridge	Cast-iron, with 7 arches supporting wooden planks & pathway; towline protective rollers missing; low iron parapets in diamond pattern in good condition
74.5	Footbridge	Cast-iron, with 4 arches supporting wooden planks; low iron parapets; plaque inscribed "Erected Anno 1800" in centre of arch on both sides; towline rod on north side only

74.6	Sydney Gardens No.1 Tunnel	Roving, highly decorated, rusticated; north portal in need of repair in places; tunnel stone throughout; many masons' marks; some patching with brick at water level; south portal plain with towpath over, good condition
74.6	Cleveland House	Stone, 3-storey; slate roof; good condition
74.7	Sydney or Pinche's Wharf	Brick, stone & clapboard; winding hole nearby
74.7	Sydney Wharf Bridge	Roving, stone, unusual ring pattern in balustrade; part badly worn; rebuilt to follow line of new road but arch original
74.8	Somerset Coal Wharf	Stone walls & buildings; corrugated asbestos roof; old wharf area now private garden
75.0	Widcombe Top Lock, No.13	Top gate o.k., offside beam broken; bottom gates o.k., but beams sawn off; stop planks in place above lock
75.0	Footbridge	Cast-iron arch over lock tail; wrought-iron handrails
75.0	Toll House	Stone, Gothic-style windows & doorway; slate roof; good condition; inhabited
75.1	Widcombe Second Lock, No.12	Top gates o.k., towpath side beam missing; offside o.k.; bottom towpath-side gate missing, offside present
75.2	Pumping Station Chimney	Stone, decorated top
75.2	Abbey View Lock, No.11	All gates & beams o.k
75.2	Horseshoe Bridge	Stone, good condition; no towpath; slopes up to road line on south side
75.3	Wash House Lock, No.10	Top gates o.k., offside beam collapsed, bottom towpath-side beam broken and gate beyond repair; other gate & beam o.k.
75.3	Wash House Footbridge	Cast-iron arches with ring pattern; iron railings, newly painted, good condition
75.4	Bridge Lock, No.9	Top gates o.k., beams beyond repair; bottom beams collapsed; towpath-side gate beyond repair; other o.k
75.4	Pulteney Road Bridge	Roving, stone, good condition
75.5	Chapel Lock, No.8	Top gates o.k., towpath-side beam missing, offside beam sawn off; bottom gates o.k.
75.5	Widcombe Lower Lock, No.7	Top gates o.k., towpath-side beam collapsed, offside one o.k.; bottom gates o.k., offside beam broken
75.5	Pumping Station	Stone with square stone chimney, slate roof; pumps removed long ago
75.5	Dolemead Bridge	Stone, good condition; no towpath through arch

Glossary

Abutment	That part of a pier or wall which sustains an arch.
Arch	Underside of standard canal brick or stone bridge.
Ashlar	Masonry walling of accurately formed and squared stones with a smooth face laid in regular courses with fine joints.
Balance beam	The beam projecting along the top of a lock gate which helps balance its weight. By pushing against its end the gate is opened or closed.
Baluster	One of a number of stone (or iron, or wood) vertical members supporting a coping or parapet.
Balustrade	A row of balusters.
Barge	Generic term for a boat measuring about 70 feet long by about 14 feet wide, as opposed to a narrow boat, which is only about 7 feet wide.
Batter	Receding concave slope of a wall from the ground upwards, narrower at the top.
Blocking course	A course of solid masonry built upon the top of a projecting cornice, which neutralises any tendency for the cornice to overturn the wall.
Bridge hole	The narrow channel where the canal is crossed by a bridge.
Buttress	Support for a wall, usually part of it.
Coping	Protective capping of brick or stone on the top of a wall.
Corbel	A stone projection built into a wall and projecting from its face as a bracket to support a beam, roof truss or cornice.
Cornice	A projecting horizontal feature, usually moulded, which crowns an external façade.
Course	A continuous layer of bricks, or stones, of equal thickness in a wall.
Culvert	The tunnel through which a stream passes under an embankment.
Cut	A boatman's name for a canal, originally an entirely artificial cut channel, as opposed to a navigable river or river navigation.
Cutwater	The rounded or V-shaped base of an arch, which protects the arch from the effects of a river in flood.
Draw	When a paddle or sluice of a lock is raised to allow water to flow through the gate.
Entablature	In classical 'orders', the three horizontal members above the supporting column(s), the lowest of which is the cornice.
Façade	The exterior front or face of a building or bridge.

Flange	Projecting flat collar with bolt holes, to enable pipes to be connected.
Flight	Series of locks following closely together, as at Devizes and Crofton.
Guttae	Wedge-shaped projections resembling tombstone teeth.
Handspike	A bar of iron, or wood tipped with iron, used as a lever to operate simple winches to open or close paddles.
Head	Of a lock, that portion immediately above the top gates.
Heel post	Vertical part of a lock gate nearest its hanging, and its axis on which the gate pivots, being rounded at the back to fit into the hollow quoin, in which it partially revolves.
Hollow quoin	The recess into which the heel post of a lock gate fits.
Intrados	The underside of an arch.
Keystone	The wedge-shaped central voussoir of an arch, usually larger than its neighbours on either side.
Leat	Open watercourse, or ditch, supplying water.
Lengthman	A canal company employee in charge of a particular length of canal.
Lintel	Piece of stone or timber laid horizontally across the top of a doorway or window to carry the walling above.
Lock	A gated chamber which enables a boat to pass from one level of the canal to another.
Lozenge	Strictly a diamond-shaped decorative figure, but sometimes used to describe an oval-shaped figure.
Moulding	An ornamental and continuous line of grooving or projections worked on a plain surface.
Narrow Boat	Canal boat measuring c.70 feet long by almost 7 feet wide.
Niche	Ornamental recess in a wall, usually with an arched top; often, but not invariably, designed to contain a statue.
Paddle	A sluice valve, by the opening or closing of which water can be let through or retained. A gate paddle is built into a lock gate and a ground paddle uses an underground culvert.
Pound	The stretch of water between two locks. The length can vary from a few feet to several miles.
Puddle	A mixture of clay, sand and water, which when kneaded makes a watertight bed for a canal.
Quoin	The large corner stone of a building, bridge or lock (see also Hollow quoin).
Rise	Of an arch, the height from the springing line to the crown.
Roving bridge	A bridge which carries the towpath from one side of the canal to the other, sometimes called a turnover bridge.

Rustication	A method of working external blocks of stone with a hammer to give an impression of great strength, the margins only being chiselled off smooth and accentuated by carefully recessed joints.
Skew arch	An arch with its axis oblique to its abutments.
Slew	Pivot to the left or right from normal forward position.
Span	The distance between the supporting abutments of an arch.
Spandrel	The quasi-triangular space between the outer curve of an arch and its enclosing rectangular moulded frame.
Springing line	The level from which an arch begins to spring, i.e. to curve inwards and upwards.
Stop gates	On long pounds, or where a breach in the canal bank would be disastrous, it is usual for stop gates, which are similar to lock gates but without balance beams, to be fitted at intervals. In the event of a serious leak, the gates are closed and the loss of water confined to that length between the two sets of stop gates.
Stop grooves	Vertical grooves into which stop planks can be inserted. They are let into the walls at locks and bridge holes, so that a temporary dam can be made in order to drain a lock or pound.
Stop planks	Stout planks with handles to enable them to be slotted easily into stop grooves.
Stoppage	The temporary closing of a canal for repairs.
Strap	A band or collar of wrought iron, which retains the heel post of a lock gate in position, while being loose enough to allow the gate to pivot.
String course	A moulding or projecting course of brickwork or stone running horizontally across the face of a building or bridge.
Summit level	The highest pound on a canal into which the main supply of water for working the locks has to be delivered.
Sump	Lowest part of a well, from which water can be pumped.
Swag	An ornamental festoon of flowers, fruit and foliage, often tied with carved ribbons, suspended at each end and hanging down in the middle: much used in Renaissance architecture.
Tail	Of a lock, that portion immediately below the bottom gates.
Truss	Triangular wooden framework supporting roof.
Turnover bridge	Bridge where the towpath changes sides, sometimes called a roving bridge.
Voussoir	One of the stones forming the outer edge of an arch. Being wedge-shaped, they make the arch self-supporting.
Winding hole	A widened place provided on a canal for turning a boat round, often near wharves. Formerly spelt 'winning' and pronounced similarly.

Bibliography

The principal works of reference used in this study were:

The Kennet & Avon Canal: Re-development Scheme (Kennet & Avon Canal Association, 1961)

Boucher, Cyril T. G. — *John Rennie 1761-1821* (Manchester University Press, 1963)

Clew, Kenneth R. — *The Kennet & Avon Canal* (David & Charles, 1968)

Hammond, Nicholas — *The Kennet & Avon Waterway: the Complete Chart* (Imray, Laurie, Norie & Wilson, Parts1-4, 1969; Parts 5-9, 1975)

Other works of reference were:

The Butty (The Kennet & Avon Canal Trust, various editions)

Claverton Pumping Station: A Definitive Study (K&ACT, 1984)

Crofton Beam Engines (The Crofton Society, 1975)

The Crofton Pumps, Savernake (Railway Enthusiasts' Club, 1958)

Allsop, Niall — *The Kennet & Avon Canal: A User's Guide* (Millstream Books, 1987; revised 1992)

Bonthron, P. — *My Holidays on Inland Waterways* (Thomas Murby & Co, 1929)

Bowyer, Valerie E. — *Along the Canal in Bath* (Kingsmead Press, 1976)

Bradley, Ian — "The Crofton Beam Engines" (*The Model Engineer*, June 1952)

Elton, Arthur — "Presidential Address: The Pre-History of Railways" (*Proceedings of the Somerset Archaeological and Natural History Society*, 1963, 31-59)

Gorham, Major — "The Kennet & Avon Canal and its Marks" (*Transactions of the Somerset Masters Lodge*, 1920, 172-182)

Hadfield, Charles — *British Canals* (Phoenix House, 1950; revised 1959)

Hadfield, Charles — *The Canals of Southern England* (Phoenix House, 1965)

Heath, Frank R. — *Wiltshire* (Little Guide series) (Methuen & Batsford, 1911; revised 1949)

McQuillan, Don — "From Brewer to Bridge Builder: reflections on the life and work of James Dredge" (*Proceedings of the Institution of Civil Engineers*, 102, February 1994, 34-42)

Rolt, L. T. C. — *The Inland Waterways of England* (George Allen & Unwin, 1950)

Smiles, Samuel — *Lives of the Engineers* (John Murray, 1862)

Torrens, Hugh — *The Evolution of a Family Firm: Stothert and Pitt of Bath* (Stothert & Pitt, 1978)

Acknowledgments

I am indebted to various people who have helped me considerably during the compilation of this book. Foremost among these is Ken Clew, who gave me several sources of reference, which subsequently proved in most cases to be veritable gold mines of information. Ken Clew was also of great help in clearing up several points that arose after I had commenced the initial draft. Then there is the late Fred Rickard, who printed approximately half the total number of photographs taken; for only a selected few, unfortunately, was there room to include in this book. Pictures of the interior of Claverton Pumping Station on pages 88 and 89 were obtained through a member of the Kennet & Avon Canal Trust, David Harris. The photo of Claverton pit wheel is used by courtesy of the K&ACT. I am very grateful to John Boucher for permission to reproduce diagrams from his father's book on John Rennie, on pages 24, 31 and 87. Also, my thanks to the K&ACT for permission to quote from *The Butty* and *The Kennet & Avon Canal Re-development Scheme*, and to reproduce the drawing of Crofton Pumping Station on page 35. Thanks go to The Railway Enthusiasts Club for the picture of the Crofton Pumping Station chimney before truncation, on page 36, and to Bath Central Library, Bath & North East Somerset Library & Archive Section, for permission to quote from Major Gorham's "The Kennet & Avon Canal and its Marks", on pages 109-110.

I am also grateful for help and information received from various people during my excursions to the canal, including the landlord of *The Bear* at Devizes, and the kind lady in the cottage near Dundas who loaned me a pair of binoculars so that I could read the inscription on the tablets mounted on the aqueduct; to friends and relatives who supplied me with cuttings and bits of information; and especially to my late mother who did all the typing for the original thesis.

More recently, I am indebted to the following who have provided invaluable information, advice and encouragement: Phil Braithwaite (two arms and a leg, page 106), Nigel Crowe, Julia Elton, Chris Gibson, John Gould, Clive Hackford, Nicholas Hammond, Ray Knowles, Barry McNeeney, Don McQuillan (in connection with James Dredge), Brian Mayland, Janet Moult, Arnold Patchett, Stella Pierce, Adrian and June Potts (for permission to use an early photograph of *The Barge*, Honeystreet, on page 49), Michael Richardson, of Richardson Reed (in connection with *Cleveland House* message hole), Sonia Rolt, Lady Rothschild of Stowell Park, Bob Scudamore, Hugh Torrens and Tim Wheeldon. Finally, there is Tim Graham of Millstream Books, without whose advice and experience this work might never have seen the light of day.

Index

This index includes the names of people and places mentioned in the text, as well as the major structures of the Kennet & Avon Canal.

All Cannings 23, 50
Allington 50
Avington 19
Avon Navigation 7-9
Avon, Bristol 7-8, 9, 64, 68, 70, 72, 74, 78, 87-8, 102, 105
Avoncliff Aqueduct 10, 72, 74-7, 93, 107-111
Barge Inn, Honeystreet 49, 50
Barge Inn, Seend 63
Barnes, Edward 25
Barton Court, Kintbury 18
Bath 7, 8, 9, 29, 91-105, 107
Bathampton 23, 90, 91, 107-8
Beehive, The, Widbrook 70
Bishop's Cannings 24, 25, 51
Biss Aqueduct 68, 74
Blackwell, John 20, 56
Blackwell, Thomas 36
Boulton & Watt 35, 36
Bradford-on-Avon 7, 70, 77, 78, 106, 110
Bridge Inn, Horton 51
Brindley, James 40
British Transport Commission 10
British Waterways Board 10
Brown, Samuel 45
Bruce, Thomas 8, 37
Bruce Tunnel 29, 37
Brunel, I. K. 45, 93
Burbage 30, 38, 48
Caen Hill 56-60
Calne 7, 9
Cherhill 7
Chippenham 7, 9
Clarke, James 11
Claverton Down 107
Claverton Pumping Station 78, 84, 86, 87-9
Cleveland House, Bath 97, 112
Coalbrookdale Company 94
Combe Down 107-8
Conkwell 85, 107-8
Crofton 27, 30, 32
Crofton Pumping Station 32, 34-6, 48
Cross Guns, The, Avoncliff 74
Darlington Wharf 91
Denford Mill 19
Devizes 8, 29, 41, 52-60, 106
Dredge, James 44-5
Dun, River 27, 28, 32
Dundas Aqueduct 8, 74, 77, 78-87, 93, 107-111
Dundas Arms, Kintbury 18
Dundas, Charles 18, 80
Dunmill 19
Fox & Co 88
Foxhangers 8, 26, 54, 106
Froxfield 27, 28, 35
Froxfield Feeder 27

George Inn, Bathampton 91
Gould, John 10, 48
Great Bedwyn 7, 8, 27, 29, 30, 39, 107
Great Western Railway 9-10, 29, 36, 64, 106, 112, 113, 115
Hamstead Marshall 14, 15
Hardy, Roger 48
Harvey & Sons 36
Hilperton Marsh 25, 67
Honeystreet 48-9
Horton 51
Hungerford 7, 8, 15, 20, 22, 25, 26, 27, 32, 64
Hutchings, Denys 48
Inland Waterways Association 10
Jessop, William 7
Kennet & Avon Canal Association 5, 48
Kennet & Avon Canal Trust 5, 24, 34, 48, 53, 57, 89
Kennet Navigation 7, 9, 20
Kennet, River 7, 14, 15, 27, 32
Kintbury 18
Lady's Bridge 46, 72, 92, 95
Ladydown Aqueduct 68
Langford, H. A. C. 38
Lacock 7
Limpley Stoke 8, 78, 107
Little Bedwyn 27
Lloyd, Ben and John 29
Marlborough 7, 8
Martinslade 63
Melksham 7, 9, 24
Milk Hill 50
Monkton Combe 106
Murhill 107-8
New Mill 41
Newbury 7, 8, 10, 11, 12, 29
Pewsey 8, 41
Pinche's or Sydney Wharf, Bath 98
Ramsbury 7
Reading 7, 9, 29
Rennie, John 7, 17, 24, 25, 30, 35, 40, 50, 68, 77, 84, 88, 90, 93, 107-8
Robbins, Lane & Pinnegar 48
Rogers, Cyril 15
Savernake 7, 38, 41
Seend 62, 63, 107
Semington 64, 65, 66, 68, 70
Sheepwash Feeder 86
Sims engine 36
Smiles, Samuel 70
Somersetshire Coal Canal 8, 9, 82
Stanton St Bernard 50
Stothert & Pitt 38, 93-4, 100-101
Stowell Park 44-5
Summerham Brook 61-2
Sydney Gardens 6, 43, 84, 91-6, 100, 108-112
Telford, Thomas 17, 45, 94
Thames, River 7, 9, 64
Thimble Mill, Bath 105
Thomas Jonathan 81
West Mills, Newbury 13
Western Canal 7, 20
White Horse Hill, Cherhill 7
Whitworth, Robert 7
Widbrook 70
Widcombe, Bath 8, 70, 99-105
Wilcot 43, 44, 46
Wilton Water 8, 32, 34
Wilts and Berks Canal 8-9, 64, 82
Woodborough Hill 48
Wootton Rivers 16, 34, 39, 40, 41
Wroughton, Lady Susannah 46